GOBLIN

ONE'S CHICKEN COOP

GOBLINPROOFING

ONE'S CHICKEN COOP

And Other Practical Advice in Our

Campaign Against the Fairy Kingdom

REGINALD BAKELEY

**FOREWORD
BY CLINT MARSH**

Conari Press

First published in 2012 by Conari Press, an imprint of
Red Wheel/Weiser, LLC

With offices at:
665 Third Street, Suite 400
San Francisco, CA 94107
www.redwheelweiser.com

Sign up for our newsletter and special offers by going to
www.redwheelweiser.com/newsletter.

ISBN: 978-1-57324-532-6

Library of Congress Cataloging-in-Publication Data available upon request

Cover design by Jim Warner
Cover photograph © TK
Interior by Kathryn Sky-Peck

Printed in the United States of America
MAL
10 9 8 7 6 5 4 3 2 1

To Holly

CONTENTS

The Fight Afield

FOREWORD

IN EACH OF OUR LIVES, there are people who change the way we look at the world around us so fundamentally that, after we meet, we wonder how we ever got by without them. For me, no one has done this quite so boldly, or with as much personal style, as the man who has penned the book you are about to read. I consider it an honor to present to you the pioneering work of iconoclastic sportsman, gentleman farmer, and idiosyncratic clairvoyant Reginald Bakeley, my guide—and now yours—

to that most fascinating and mysterious of other-worlds: the Fairy Kingdom.

My introduction to Mr. Bakeley came about not over fireside brandies at the social club, nor was it in the early morning mist before setting out for, as Reginald would say, "a spot of gnoming" (an activity you will learn about very soon). Instead, our first meeting was under more prosaic circumstances and in the most unlikely of places—the folklore stacks of my hometown library in rural Iowa. A fervent scholar of fairy lore from a young age, I scoured any books I could find about Faerie, that golden kingdom just beyond our everyday reach, home to elves, goblins, trolls, and other representatives of "the goodpeople." Reginald's name was included in one book's footnotes discussing modern-day writers who possessed "the Second Sight," the seemingly magical ability to see and hear fairies. I was intrigued, so I copied his name into my notes.

Guided by the scant few writings of Bakeley's I could find, along with the rare interviews he granted on his life and work, I began to piece together a picture of this decidedly odd Welshman. The more I learned about him, the more fascinated I became. I was determined to meet Reginald, and following a slow and patchy correspondence, we did eventually get together during one of his visits to the United States. We met for sandwiches at a café in Berkeley, and Reginald ate and spoke with the same unbridled gusto which I would find he brought to everything in his life.

Two truths became clear to me almost immediately during that initial conversation. The first was that a life among the fairies wasn't necessarily without its troubles. Reginald was a man who, unlike other writers on the subject, had no wish to go further *into* Faerie, but was determined to fight tooth and nail to get *out*. To him, there was nothing "good" about the goodpeople. According to Reginald, the fairies of myth and folklore are not only real, but also in fact at the root of nearly every problem imaginable. Not that he was happy to let the matter rest at that. I was in the presence of a consummate clairvoyant who used his gift of Second Sight not only to *see* fairies, but to . . . well, you're about to find out how he uses it.

The second truth was that Reginald was far too busy to include any new people in his life unless they benefited his work. Instead of risking losing our nascent friendship, I offered to help him distribute his writings in America. He agreed, and we began publishing pamphlets of his "practical fairy lore" to a growing readership.

Reginald's startlingly direct guidelines on the hows and whys of ridding the chicken coop of migrating goblins, or of hunting "bothersome and delicious" gnomes, became instant favorites of everyone I showed them to, so much so that we have long hoped to gather them, along with other essays and stories, into a single volume.

And now, here it is. Those of you already familiar with Reginald's work may consider this book a long-awaited expansion of his singular vision. If you're new to this most peculiar of fairy folklorists, then he and I both wish you welcome. For those in search of a way into the Fairy Kingdom, as I was so many years ago, nothing beats the direct approach. Step aside as Reginald Bakeley kicks down the door and ushers you in with a fanfare.

— CLINT MARSH

"WHY FAERIE NEEDS HUNTING," A MANIFESTO

Up the airy mountain,

    Down the rushy glen

We daren't go a-hunting

    For fear of little men;

Wee folk, good folk,

    Trooping all together;

Green jacket, red cap,

    And white owl's feather!

         — WILLIAM ALLINGHAM

A PRETTY BIT OF DOGGEREL, that poem, and more devious than it first appears. "Daren't go a-hunting," indeed! If we follow the advice of Mr. Allingham and other weak-constitutioned fairy sympathisers, then the whole of the outdoors will soon be snatched away from mankind, its rightful master.

Whilst this cowardly little verse is right in characterising fairies as dangerous, the properly equipped and educated person is one able to move through life free from such fear and trepidation. I have made it my life's work to show how this may be done.

Thankfully, not all authors and anthropologists on the subject of Faerie share Allingham's pessimistic outlook. But among those unafraid of Faerie (by which I mean the Fairy Kingdom and all its inhabitants, from the most miniscule flower-fairy to the most towering troll), many go a bit too far, stripping away all of the fey's instinctual wickedness and presenting them as nonthreatening storybook characters.

This error, sadly, is as deadly as it is common. By treating the topic of Faerie too lightly, these chroniclers may unwittingly lead innocent people straight into the hands of mankind's greatest oppressor. The fey are not gentle creatures but malevolent meddlers, each of them in its own way. If they are to be "sugar-coated," let it be after they are first bagged and roasted.

There are other snares as well. Most writers on Faerie make the mistake of distancing their stories from the lives of their readers. Their tales are prone to be placed in a long-ago setting, a century or more into the past. Or they may be accounts from a far-off place, somewhere so exotic we might believe anything could be possible. This is misleading in the extreme, for as you will learn, the fey are not a relic of history. They truly are everywhere, from the brownie mucking up the kitchen of one's London flat to the flying horrors haunting the Scottish Highlands. They generally keep out of sight, but under the cover of darkness, or when our backs are turned, they do everything in their power to upset the tranquillity of day-to-day life.

Another misguided concept, spread mainly through popular legend, is that fairies are a vanishing facet of Nature and mankind should elevate them and respect them to a debilitating degree. Take gnomes, for example. Mindless readers of the propaganda which passes for folklore today have been brainwashed into believing that gnomes are benign spirits of the forest. "They're natural," these hapless scholars tell us. This argument never fails to send a shudder through my frame. As an inveterate outdoorsman, I believe myself eminently qualified to declare what is and what is not natural. Trees are natural. Streams are natural. Sparrows and hedgehogs and trout are natural. What is *not* natural is some little twerp of a red-capped manikin traipsing about wagging his beard and spouting rhymes, intent on harming people who'd simply like to enjoy a walk out of doors!

Finally there are the most hopeless of the lot, those who claim fairies don't exist at all. They believe

all of life's calamities can be chalked up to one's own clumsiness or simply to ill luck. This, my friends, is exactly what the fairies would like us to think.

Whether or not one "believes" in them, fairies do exist. The proof lies in the mountains of first-hand evidence I have gathered regarding the habits and predilections of every species of fey known to man. Not a single one of them have I found to be completely free of malice. And whilst some fairies, under the right circumstances, can be surprisingly useful to us (and others can be downright scrumptious), on

the whole they are entirely without merit and many of them are positively bent on making our lives miserable. It makes no difference to me whether this or that fairy is designated a member of the beneficent "Seelie Court" or to its dark, "Unseelie" counterpart. I do not make distinctions based on the personal allegiances of individual fairies. All are suspect.

Anyone who has spent more than two moments in my presence knows that I am not one merely to sit around and complain about this or that injustice. When I see something needs to be done, I snap to attention and do it. It is time we shone a lantern on the fairies, exposing them as the meddlers they are. It is time we took steps towards restoring order to our world. Anyone who would defend the Fairy Kingdom as harmless or meek is at best misinformed, and at worst, an enemy.

My intention has been to contribute to the discussion on Faerie a book which is *instructive*. Too many books are full of folklore and anecdote but fall flat when it comes to helping readers apply such information to everyday life. This is the first *thoroughly practical* book compiled not from second- and third-hand sources but rather from the collected wisdom of a lifetime with the accursed Second Sight. One of the few comforts this affliction affords me is that I might share with you methods and techniques to employ in our mutual campaign against the machinations of the Fairy Kingdom.

I have arranged this book into two sections. The first is written to help you in noticing fairy activity in and around the home. The second section is meant to prepare you for the possibility of fairy assault during your excursions into the countryside. In addition to the practical articles in each section, I have included a few recollections of my own fairy encounters. These are meant to serve as illustration and to remind us that even the utmost in preparation and foreknowledge is sometimes not enough to prevent mishap at the hands of the fey. It is an unfortunate truth, but not one so dire that we should give up our resistance.

I believe strongly that with sufficient knowledge of fairies and their habits, along with this or that everyday household object, even the blindest of fairy seers will possess everything needed to confront these dreadful creatures head-on. I don't pretend to have laid out an all-inclusive system for any of the pastimes I write about in this collection—hunting, farming, marriage—but hope merely to bridge a long-neglected gap. My desire is that with *Goblinproofing One's Chicken Coop*, you will be set on the path to achieving your goals in all these areas and more.

The notion that we need fear the Fairy Kingdom and its inhabitants is absurd. It is time instead that they feared us. Not only do we *dare* go a-hunting, but we declare open season on every last blackguard of a fairy who would stand between us and our dreams for a peaceful life.

Therefore, in unlocking the miniature treasure chest of practical wisdom contained within this book, I present to you my own ditty, a bit of a battle-cry, as a counterblast against Allingham's craven verse. Perhaps it will inspire you and come to serve as a source of strength in your own noble struggle against the Fairy Kingdom:

Open up each window,
    Throw wide every door
Announce to all the fairies
    We're slaves to them no more;
Brownies, pixies,
    Goblins, elves, and gnomes;
Hear our cry, begone at once,
    You shan't destroy our homes!

Ascending craggy hillside,
    Strolling country lane
No fairy makes us tremble
    Come dark or wind or rain;
Your schemes will come to nothing,
    Your plots will go nowhere;
Our wits are sharp, our senses keen,
    And we're loaded for bugbear!

— YOURS SINCERELY,
REGINALD BAKELEY

goblinproofing one's chicken coop

For Hearth & Home

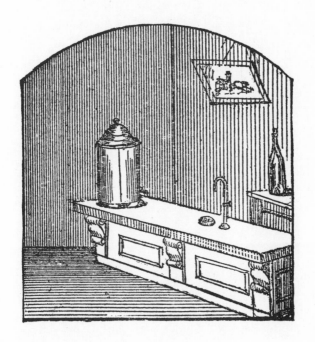

FIRST PRINCIPLES
OF FAERIE

The Pernicious Pervasiveness of Faerie •
The Brownie: A Misunderstood Fairy •
Its Ambitions • The Boggart • Finding Its Lair
and Motives • Methods of Routing •
A Sample Letter • Maelstrom

SEEN FROM THE OUTSIDE, the life of a dashing country gentleman such as myself must look like an endless parade of pleasure. Whilst I'll admit that this observation is fundamentally true, there isn't a single activity—no pheasant shoot, no cricket match, no afternoon of riverbank angling—that is not saturated with potential interference from that most ancient and insufferable people, the fairies. Perhaps the most unsettling quality of these so-called "goodpeople" is how they have insinuated themselves into every aspect of daily life. Far from being content to contain their caperings to the sylvan grove, nor to halt their march at the front gate or flower bed, these bogeys of childhood nightmare and adult paranoia are to be found nearly anywhere one might cast a glance. In my own life, the fairies and their mischievous pranks have caused me no end of trouble, scaring off my entire household staff, souring many of my closest friendships, and exacting unwanted expense and worry until all I'm left with are a few tattered scraps of sanity. These I raise as war banner against the fey. I beseech you to rally beside me.

Of all the innumerable types of fairies, the one most commonly encountered, yet also the most commonly misunderstood, is the brownie. Here is a nocturnal fairy "helper" who stands no taller than the spout of one's teapot, yet is able to single-handedly carry out an astonishing number of household tasks. Renowned historically for its knack for churning butter and grinding wheat into flour, the modern brownie has mastered a repertoire revolving around pressed laundry and freshly brewed cups of tea. In exchange for its labour, it might skim a dram of milk from the bottle or gnaw the occasional simple crust of bread.

It sounds pleasant enough, having one of these magnificently industrious creatures scampering about, but the household harbouring a brownie would do better to consider itself not blessed but beset.

I say "beset" because in truth the brownie is nothing but a ruthless social climber. In the mists of antiquity, brownies were simple spirits of the earth. Yet as civilisation grew, these ambitious fairies hitched a ride, haunting hearthstones and lurking in linen baskets, biding their time until they themselves could have proper houses of their own. Now these jealous creatures live in a limbo-land between the Fairy Kingdom and our own world, residents of both places but full citizens of neither. By serving us endless cups of tea and pressing our clothes into immaculate crispness, they hope to ingratiate themselves upon us. They hope to become, in a word, men.

This is a preposterous state of affairs.

Even though the brownies are ignorant of their rightful place, I could almost be persuaded to adopt them into the fold; they're that fantastically useful. What stays my heart, though, is the brownie's fatal flaw—bitterness. Eons of toil have built up a terrible supply of enmity in them, and this much rage, condensed into the brownie's tiny frame, is little more than a powder keg, one sporting the shortest of fuses. The brownie is a learned scholar of its own twisted version of etiquette, and the slightest affront to its sensibilities can send it into a murderous rage, twisting its form into that of the monstrous *boggart*, as destructive as the brownie is helpful. Whilst a home hosting a brownie lodger may be the picture of comfort and peace, the coming of the boggart is the undoing of all of this and is as disquieting as a herd of wild boars let loose in the parlour.

So should you awaken one morning to discover an unexplained cup of impeccably brewed tea atop your kitchen counter or slide open your dresser drawer to find a stack of perfectly ironed handkerchiefs, rejoice not. Instead, I urge you to commence with the following sequence of proven countermeasures. The brownie depends upon your gratitude, and the more of its ingratiating favours you allow yourself, the more difficult it will be to rid your home of the sycophantic squatter, who will inevitably transform and throw into turmoil all you have worked so hard to achieve.

Firstly, you must locate precisely where in your household the brownie has set up residence. Brownies are at the bottom of the barrel figuratively and quite often literally. Upturn your entire home until you find its hidey-hole. Open all the kitchen cabinets and pull out their contents, especially from seldom-used cupboards. Worry not about upsetting the brownie in his lair. If he hears you coming, he will flee in modesty and shame, hoping that you will overlook his home.

The purpose of this search is not to catch the brownie but rather to see exactly *what* his aspirations are. A miniature dormitory set up in the back of a cupboard may be recognised by a doll's house bed and tiny grass mat arranged in mock domesticity by the brownie. Once you find them, look more closely. What you are after are *details*. A framed Queen's-head postage stamp or a coronation tea cup now employed as a bathtub indicates you've got a miniscule royalist in your midst. A preserved dragonfly or a stuffed shrew shows up the work of a budding naturalist. Quickly take a series of mental notes and be careful not to disturb anything you chance upon. You wish only to observe and depart, before the brownie musters the courage to return and sees what you're up to.

Once you have determined to your satisfaction the particular longings of your household's ambitious stowaway, you are ready to take real steps towards its removal. And how is a brownie infestation such as this best handled, you may ask? Perhaps with poison, traps, or dogs? These are all perfectly effective methods against lesser vermin, but none of them are sufficient to withstand the wrath of the boggart. What this situation calls for is tact, cunning, and above all, kindness, even if it is the sort which is only feinted at.

The way to deal with any such freeloader is to thank him overmuch, to play on his insecurities and let him know, in a roundabout way, that he has no hope of ever escaping his Faerie origins and joining the world of men, at least not in this household. Get thee to a tailor, my friend, and take a brownie-sized doll with you. Commission a suit of clothing perfect for your brownie's interests, the more formal or comprehensive the better. Does he fancy himself an equestrian, for example? A hacking jacket and a pair of riding breeches are required. If your brownie possesses mountaineering leanings, a Tyrolean sports coat and a tidily spooled length of twine are the beginning elements of a smart Alpiner costume.

Once complete, the outfit should be brought home wrapped in paper so as to be safe from prying brownie eyes. Keep it within view as you prepare the second half of your remedy and the clincher: the effusive letter of thanks.

I'll admit that the composition of this letter calls for some strength of will in order to keep your writing hand from going into spasms, but remember there are times in life when sentiment trumps sincerity and this is one of them. Aim to flatter, yes, but with full indication that *you recognise the brownie as a brownie*, not as the man it wishes to be. I give here an example of how to compose one such letter. Use it as you will, or not—I'm sure your own situation will call for a letter with its own particular flavour.

Estimable House Brownie
Back Corner
Pan Cabinet
Kitchen
Bakeley Hall
Pembrokeshire, Wales

My dear Mr. Brownie,

Since you've come to stay, the house has positively gleamed with cleanliness and good cheer. Oh, to think I've got my very own fairy! It's such a pleasure to know you're around. I must be imagining the wee tinkle of bells, so unobtrusive are you as you prepare such unparalleled cups of tea. And the pocket handkerchiefs! Never before have they enjoyed such crisp creases.

I've told everyone I know what good fortune it is to have a little fairy all to myself. My only regret is that I can't repay you with more than this new suit of clothes for your days off, when you are free to trundle about and play at your little "man" activities. So charming and quaint! Thank you, thank you twenty times over, you diligent and amusing creature!

Yours sincerely,
Reginald Bakeley

In my experience it is easier to write such a letter whilst biting into an old belt, although this can get in the way of the oft-consulted whisky tumbler. I trust you'll find the way that works best for you.

Fold the letter into an envelope addressed to the brownie and place it, along with the wrapped suit of clothes, just outside his lair. Then hurry, because the clock is ticking and you have only until nightfall to secure your home against the coming tempest. Swing open the front door of the house and stow any fine china or irreplaceable heirlooms in your bedchambers. Lock yourself in there as well and try, just try, to get to sleep that night. I venture to say you'll have a devil of a time drifting off, as at any minute the brownie will emerge from his hidey-hole to try on the clothes and read the letter. It is then but a matter of seconds before the reaction. The astute brownie will realise it has no chance of ever being anything but a fairy in your eyes and, transforming into the boggart and hurling invectives and whatever household objects are not tied down, will storm out the open door, never to return. Should your brownie not be bright enough to understand your meaning, he will delight in the gift and simply set off on a new life with his dashing set of clothing, confident he has at last "arrived."

In either case, the bounder is gone. Restore your house to order, throw out all the little furnishings in the brownie's lair, and give the cupboard a proper scrubbing. Your life and your home are once more your own. Brew yourself a cup of tea and smile, for you have reclaimed the first crucial piece of territory in your fight against the meddling antics of the fey.

GOBLINPROOFING ONE'S CHICKEN COOP

The Gentlemanly Art of Chickenry • What Are Goblins? • The Vileness of Changeling Eggs • Goblin Migrations • Ley Lines and Ley Markers • De-Sanctification

SURELY THERE IS NO PURSUIT more reward-ing than the gentlemanly art of chickenry. For a minor initial investment an individual can provide boundless meat and eggs for himself and his family, and will reap the benefits of a natural alarm clock in the form of the rooster's crow at dawn. The dark forces of the fey never truly let man rest, however, and the threat of a goblin intrusion into the hen cottage is a danger which can destroy a fine coop, its residents, and the very will of the farmer. But a few simple checks and alterations to your existing chicken coop can keep it and its plucky cluckers secure against this unbearable prospect.

Goblins are the marauding vagabonds of the Fairy Kingdom, roving alone or in mobs from town to town. They relish upsetting the sensibilities of man and fairy alike with their crass ways. Goblins love to eat eggs and delight in using them in pranks, and they are known to lodge in chicken coops in two ways: as willing tenants or as changelings. The former either wander into the hen cottage and decide to stay or in some instances are trapped, the mechanics of which I will explain shortly. The latter — changelings — are swapped during their goblin infancy for a hen of your own. Both types of goblin are hazardous, as they will grow into warped versions of your hens if left in the coop. Aside from the peril presented by their eggs, which they do indeed begin to lay after a short while, goblin hens are notorious for their tempers, which are nearly as quick as their razor-sharp beaks.

To keep goblins from approaching your hen cottage voluntarily, it is advisable to keep the place as tidy as possible. A thorough cleaning every two weeks will maintain your chickens' happiness and health, and will repel potential miscreants from calling the little house their own, as goblins prefer dwellings similar to the murky, filthy caves of their own kingdom.

Nothing spoils a carefully prepared breakfast like the cracking of a changeling egg. Whilst so many of these dangerous ovoids look and feel perfectly normal, they possess repulsive qualities seldom noticed until mealtime. Some are filled with maggots, others with blood. There are reports of changeling eggs as hard as concrete and others which explode when broken. A few have beautiful shells which hatch tuberculosis and smallpox.

The Ungerslud family of Shropshire was the unlucky recipient of a goblin curse via changeling eggs, for the morning after the eggs were eaten, the lot of them awoke with their legs on backwards, as they remain today. Young Ettie Ungerslud went on to become a source of local pride by clinching the National Backwards Hopscotch Championship later that year, but surely you can imagine that life is not all fun and games under such a curse.

In all honesty, it's not always the goblin's fault when it becomes trapped in a chicken coop. Being a stubborn and rather stupid lot, goblins are not able to change their course unless sensibly advised. And so it is not uncommon that, when travelling from place to place, these nomadic scoundrels enter into structures from which, according to their own obstinate logic, there is no escape. A small crack between the planks of the east-facing wall of the coop, for example, will trap any goblin coming from that direction unless there is a corresponding gap on the west side.

A chicken farmer in St. Leonards Grange, on England's southern coast, once discovered a goblin in his coop. When the surprised rustic asked the goblin whence it came, it responded, "From the far, far north." To the question of "And where are you going?" the inmate replied, "To the far, far south." Indeed, upon inspection the farmer found a minor crevice in the northern wall of the coop and none in the south. Wise to the goblin's ways, the farmer kindly offered to pry a plank from the south wall to free him, but warned him that there was nothing in that direction but the cold dark sea. The grateful intruder admitted that he had no idea he would have leapt into the ocean with his next steps and asked the farmer if there was anything he could do to repay the favour.

goblinproofing one's chicken coop

The simpleton thought for a long while, as one does when granted a fairy wish, and finally decided that the goblin should marry his daughter, who was very ugly and more trouble than she was worth. The goblin agreed happily and took the horrified, screaming girl with him on his way back to the northern coast. The farmer breathed a sigh of relief, knowing that life would be good from then on, his breakfasts safe from repulsive changeling eggs.

Ley lines are channels of energy which run along the surface of the earth, tracing connecting pathways between stone circles, burial mounds, and other particular geographical features and man-made edifices. Fairies of all sorts, including goblins, use them as a network of highways, and if your chicken coop happens to rest upon one of these channels, then my fine fellow, it's only a matter of time before you acquire your first changeling hen.

Every chickener should check his hen cottage's location and ensure it is not built on a ley line. On a cloudless day, climb to the roof of the coop and point the tail end of its weathervane in the precise direction of the nearest site of ancient and mysterious origin. If there is no such place in sight as you stand atop the roof, get down and, with the help of a map and the following list of ley markers from Alfred Watkins's *The Old Straight Track*, find the most significant example nearest your farm.

Watkins's List of Ley Markers, in Descending Importance

- Mounds (burial mounds and similar earthworks)

- Stones (megaliths of various description)

- Circular Moats

- Castles

- Traditional Wells

- Early Churches

- Crossroads

- Road Alignments (especially those longer than 1½ miles)

- Notched Fords

- Un-Notched Fords

goblinproofing one's chicken coop

- Tree Groups (particularly those atop named hills)

- Ancient, Named Trees

- Hillside Notches

- Track Junctions

- Camps or Hill-Forts

- Ponds

- Square Moats

In his *Mythology of the British Isles*, Geoffrey Ashe notes that hillside figures such as the chalk horses of Uffington and Cherill have recently been added to the bottom of the list. As such, these are fine for you to use, at a pinch.

Return to the roof. Once the weathervane is positioned with tail feathers pointing towards the ascertained ley marker, squat down and align your gaze in the *opposite* direction, along the path of the weathervane's

arrow. If along its line you see or note on your map anything listed above, be it well or moat, notch or mound, then you are advised straightaway to fashion for your coop a doormat which reads, "WELCOME, SPRITES!" for you will soon be entertaining such guests. Researchers have concluded that ley lines can at times be quite broad, stretching miles across, and dowsers have determined that ley lines sometimes have a slight curve to them. Allowing an extra ten degrees to either side of your weathervane arrow's path may therefore give you a clearer sense of your coop's susceptibility to changelings.

Apart from leaving the door to your coop open at night (which would clear out chickens both changeling and standard) or the costly solution of constructing a coop entirely of iron (which is as good as poison to the goblins), there isn't much one can do with the structure itself to keep the rogues from setting up camp. One must either move to a new farm in disgrace, or — and you might like to sit down before reading this — divert the ley.

Some readers might think that going to the bother of constructing a new ley marker an appropriate number of miles distant from one's farm is a rash step in their work to thwart the goblins. It is actually not as outlandish a proposal as it first sounds, and I will explain why. Think of a new ley marker as you do your chicken coop. It is a structure that costs something to build, is relatively inexpensive to maintain, and provides advantages to future generations. One must take the long view when envisioning such things. Foremost, it diverts the ley line, curving it around your farm and leaving you safeguarded against goblins. Furthermore, a new site will bring additional commerce to your town in the form of holiday-seekers. To maximise potential profit at your farm stand, commission and stock souvenir egg cups emblazoned with a painting of the new ley marker.

If you are not already volunteering for your town council, now is the time to begin. Within the space of a few years, you will undoubtedly have the clout necessary to secure a site and successfully petition for a government grant to fund construction. In many towns the local chapter of the Freemasons is more than capable of building a qualifying ley marker. Because of the fraternity's interest in ancient mysteries and the order's roots in construction, not

to mention its core precepts of charity and brotherhood, such a task is well in keeping with Masonic
ideals. The occasional delivery of fresh eggs to the
lodge hall should be enough to establish initial relations. All that is required once you've secured their
aid is an idea of which sort of site to construct and
a certain amount of cash. Brotherhood or not, stone
circles and the like are not built on the cheap. The
secretary of your local chapter can provide you
with a list comparing types of sites and their prices.
Choose from Watkins's list one of greater impor-
tance than the site nearest your farm. Building a
site of lesser grandeur will not bend the ley, and no
ley line worth its salt will be going out of its way to

goblinproofing one's chicken coop

align with a scruffy little chalk horse. Make it grand. Costs vary between lodges and depend somewhat on the season, but any price seems reasonable once you've spent a few moments thinking of the resulting benefits.

In the event you've gone all out and piled up a fully featured burial mound stocked with its own assortment of ancient kings and venerable artifacts, then you ought to feel practically pulled towards the new ley marker yourself — along with all the dark fey and day-trippers — so powerful is its eerie gravity. Well done. If, however, your site falls more than a few places down Watkins's list, it is best to go one step further and have it *de-sanctified*. This

necessary procedure begins a flow of unnatural energy which will attract the goblins away from your farm. And this, sadly, is where real expenditure comes in. Petition the bishop of your diocese for an official certificate of de-sanctification. Bribery is not out of the question in these cases, and bishops aren't going to settle for the occasional bucket of eggs, either. As a bargaining point in the negotiations, it can prove beneficial to remind the bishop that the upturn in tourism may increase his flock. Even with this in mind, one should be prepared to spend roughly twice the rate of construction for a proper de-sanctification.

Once all is squared up, the last body to hire will be that of the dowser who, forked stick wavering before him, can verify with certainty that the ley line has in fact curved around your plot. Go to bed early, my happy friend, and rise at dawn to gather eggs from your freshly goblinproofed chicken coop.

A GROUNDSKEEPER'S GUIDE TO DWARFS

A Non-Native Species • Dwarfish History •
Rustics and Cider • Dwarfspotting •
Stones vs. Stumps • Keep Calm and Carry Off
• Where Help May Be Found •
The Opportunity for Initiation

LEAVING OFF FROM the hen cottage, the groundskeeper on a de-goblinised estate daren't step too many paces into the barnyard and surrounding fields without keeping an eye open for signs of at least one other unwelcome and meddlesome creature, a non-native species which has gained a substantial foothold in Britain's rich soil over the centuries. Any hope of employing the common fey deterrent of iron against this foe will prove fruitless, as iron is its foremost trade. We speak in hushed tones of the squinty-eyed metalworker of legend: the dwarf.

Due to its sly shape-shifting ability, the dwarf is likely to go unnoticed on the modern estate. Seen in its natural form, it resembles one of your sturdier yet stunted crofters glimpsed at the village pub, dour face speckled with soot from a day's toil at the forge, grey beard streaked with ale from an evening spent recuperating. Unlike men, however, these grimy urchins are active primarily at night, spending the daylight hours in underground homes or on the topsoil in the form of stones or tree stumps.

It has not always been so. From the time of their ancient forging of legendary wonders such as Thor's hammer *Mjöllnir*, the dwarfs were no villains but rather in fact the most helpful servants to gods and men, clanging about in their smithies as they hammered molten metal into enchanted swords for the aristocracy and perfectly wrought horseshoes for the common people. Their subterranean cities were marvels of stonecraft and construction, carved out from mountain roots by honest industry and the dwarfs' eldritch ability to fashion rock, soil, and iron to their then-noble will. The tragic fall of King Arthur ushered in the twilight of this golden era. It was then that Merlin, the greatest magician of all time, charged the dwarfs with ceaseless toil at their anvils such that they might stock the most magnificent armory ever known, one which would await the king's eventual triumphant return.

While it's true that the dwarfs of yore are thus bound to work to this day to craft peerless sword, helm, and shield, their descendants, tragically forgotten in Merlin's mutterings, are under no such contract. Purposeless, lusty, and nigh on immortal, the dwarfish population has multiplied with each generation, finally bursting the bounds of its underground halls. Emerging blinking and aimless, the dwarfs now wander the countryside—slowly and in an ungainly manner, to be sure—plopping down occasionally in the form of stone or stump for "naps," which can last for years. In these inanimate, unproductive forms, the dwarfs block the goodman's plough, mar otherwise unspoilt vistas, and literally stand in the way of progress towards an era when mankind, not some squat mockery of it, can be said to have the upper hand. Worse than the sleeping dwarf is the roused one, who thinks nothing of carelessly using his magic to warp the foundations of nearby stone cottages or to strew sharp swords and cart-endangering helms (albeit of unsurpassed craftsmanship) about the farmer's fields.

Dwarfspotting

It is therefore important for the groundskeeper to maintain a watchful eye on the arrangement of stones and tree stumps on the estate. This can be aided by historical maps of the property which indicate such details, yet this approach is no match for qualified, able-bodied help. Judge not the itinerant, goggle-eyed rustic who, taking a respite from his labours, is to be found gazing for hours at the odd standing stone or misshapen oak stump. In fact, befriend him.

These countryside wanderers may seem as directionless and undesirable as the dwarfs themselves, but are in sooth guardians of the glebe who can provide an invaluable service to the groundskeeper. An afternoon's ration of cider is a small price to pay one of these rural sages in exchange for a consultation regarding the finer points of their observation technique.

Any unfamiliar stone (alone or in formation) which you or your pastoral mentor lays suspicion upon may be a dwarf *incognito*. A test against this sort of trickery involves dislodging the stone to check the underside for any unmetamorphosed bits of the fairy. This is not an inconsiderable task, as dwarf-stones can weigh in at well over the heft of a full-grown man. Brace yourself with a few mouthfuls of the cider and remember to crouch low when lifting the stone, you and the rustic working as one man. With stone safely resting on its side, commence your investigation. The most obvious clue that your stone may in fact be a dwarf will be the presence of one or two stout fingers emerging from its base, caked in soil as if after a morning's dig in the veg patch. By not attaining a complete transformation, the dwarf maintains contact with the earth, the primary source of all its dark magic and unearthly vitality. Never fall victim to the dwarf's not uncommon ruse of changing into a woodland creature *and then* into a stone. If the investigator, be he proper groundskeeper or simple countryside tinker, catches sight of a hare's ear or a toad's back leg dangling from the base of an upturned stone, it is no less a sign of malicious fey activity than would be a few hirsute knuckles emerging from the same.

Keep Calm and Carry Off

It is only natural that one may react with alarm or disgust when confronted the first time with such a monstrosity as a befingered stone, but placidity of mind and action must be maintained at all costs. *Do not touch* the yet-dwarfish bits of the stone. To do so will awaken the creature and stir up its innate tendency towards bloodthirsty revenge. A dislodged dwarf is a disturbed dwarf, but a damaged dwarf is a dwarf dishonoured, and if there is evidence of a fairy with a looser grasp on the concepts of either "forgive" or "forget," my extensive research and experience have not yet brought it to light. The gravest crimes against dwarf-stones have involved communities of well-meaning but foolish people who, employing alternately bonfires and dousings of cold water, have caused the stones to crack into pieces small enough for reassignment into the construction of unwittingly macabre village buildings

goblinproofing one's chicken coop

and bridges. It is against my reserved nature to go into detail about the vengeful actions carried out against these hopeless families by the relations of the deposed dwarfs. Some such towns yet await the arrival of these enraged descendants. Woe unto them for the doom they have awakened.

Therefore, one endeavours in this situation not to harm but merely to displace the dwarf. A dwarf-stone held aloft for too long will wither its inhabitant, so a new resting place must be found. If the relocation process will be a swift one, the only precaution is to avoid human contact with the appendages. For displacement procedures taking more than a day or two, the groundskeeper is advised to pack a good amount of damp soil carefully around the entirety of the protruding parts. The dwarf won't have much of an idea that it has been found out unless it discovers that its connection to the earth has vanished, a perception which can take a few days to formulate, the slug's pace of the dwarf's intellect slowed even more by its lithic form. This time is best spent by the resolute groundskeeper and his mumbling companion in depositing the stone far from the farm, for once the dwarf awakens, it will undoubtedly be in a foul state of mind and attempt to injure its captor through bites, kicks, and practised blows of any handy tools of its vigorous trade. Even if such an attack is defended against before the dwarf wobbles off, the transgressor's identity is bound to be recorded in the dwarf's black-book compendium of enemies once he reaches home, an entry wherein spells disaster for the groundskeeper's family for generations to come.

The dwarf-stone may be set down outside the borders of the groundskeeper's estate, across the hedgerow separating his field from the neighbour's, but forethought is rewarded when contemplating this tactic. Does the groundskeeper wish to avoid the enmity not only of the dwarf but also that of his fellow man? If the answer is affirmative, other solutions must be considered. Dropping the unwitting dwarf-stone down a mineshaft or into the centre of a lake (tipplers should take care not to tip the rowboat) are two of the best remedies, for neither environment will cause the dwarf undue harm. It will feel quite at home in the shaft and will not drown underwater. Moreover, any subterranean or submerged relocation has the added benefit of securing anonymity for the groundskeeper—stones have no eyes—maintaining his safety against the dwarf's revenge.

More sinisterly clever dwarfs mould themselves to the shape of gnarled tree stumps in an effort to more thoroughly embed themselves in the landscape. The groundskeeper must exercise additional caution when investigating a stump he suspects to be a transformed dwarf, as the folds of the bark may conceal an eyelid which may open to allow the dwarf to see him, or a spiteful mouth which can shout an alarm to the dwarf's loyal brethren. What's more, the roots travel far beneath the surface of the ground and are too entwined for safe extrication. When such an enchanted tree stump is found, I'm afraid there is very little the average groundskeeper can do about it on his own.

No, dwarf-stumps must be dealt with using manners and ways known to scant few, by persons with a lifetime of training and experience tucked safely beneath their natural-fibre belt. Thankfully, there is a class of man whose numbers have kept pace with those of the dwarfs, growing especially prevalent over the past hundred years or so. Each wise worker who walks this path possesses the knowledge of the uses of holly, juniper, and mugwort, along with a pedigree traceable — often quite plainly in his grove's oral history — directly back to that utmost and aforementioned enchanter, Merlin. You know of whom I speak. Enter the Druid.

To be found at Stonehenge at the solstices and at incense-wafted bookstores and hobby shops the rest of the year, the Druid is, to a tee, your man for extracting a dwarf-stump from your property. Seek

goblinproofing one's chicken coop

him out. Offer him mead. Compliment his robes and sickle. Tell him I sent you.

As the maintainers of magical tradition, the Druids employ arcane ways to protect field and farmstead from the depredations of dwarfs. Their methods are those of what is known as *sympathetic magic*. By "sympathetic" one should not infer that the outcome of such sorceries is of a harmonious nature to the dwarf. Nothing could be further from the truth. What is sympathetic about the magic is that the actions taken by the Druid on a small scale are reflected in the larger scheme of things. A poppet may be sewn to portray the already manikin-like dwarf, for example. Once ensorcelled by the Druid, this doll may be manipulated, even reasoned with to an extent, leading in most cases to the dwarf's ungrumbling and voluntary wandering off.

The groundskeeper needs to bear in mind that while it is fine for him to observe the Druid's spell-casting (to the extent this priest of the earth allows), for goodness' sake he should not attempt these magical workings himself without proper accreditation. The Druid will likely be happy to lead you to a nearby bit of parkland for an initiation into these mysteries. But honestly, who's got the time for it? After all, there is much work to be done around the estate now that all the dwarfs are haunting the neighbour's fields or resting peacefully in the depths of a nearby coalmine or pond.

THE SECOND-SIGHT SMALLHOLDER

Standard Livestock • Seelie Livestock •
Keener's Tale • The Proper Pasture •
Appropriate Housing • Allies and Upkeep •
Generosity and Its Rewards

ANY NUMBER OF RESOURCES exists for the industrious person who wishes to take the idea of a kitchen garden or family veg patch a step further and, with the addition of a few pigs or one or more cows, establish a proper personal farm or smallholding. What is not so common on the small farmer's bookshelf is a practical guide for successfully incorporating animal members of the Fairy Kingdom into such a scheme. Intrepid "Second-Sight smallholders" may consider this essay the remedial text.

If you have not just thrown this book across the room but hold it yet with quavering hands, I commend you. If you have recently returned to it following an anguished bout of confusion and several restorative nips of whisky, I understand. For me to put forth instruction not in beating back the fey but in embracing them as an integral part of the barnyard must look like an admission of defeat.

It is not, and I shall open your eyes as to why.

Anyone with proper tools and knowledge, a modicum of courage, and a love of labour rewarded can incorporate fairy livestock into an established smallholding without harm to its existing productivity. In my experience, I have come to realise that the primary distinction between standard and seelie livestock rearing is mainly a simple matter of *scale*. Done correctly, in fact, the additions can even bolster your farm's worth, with tiny fey cattle grazing upon pastures too small for standard livestock to reach.

Of course there is the matter of procuring the fairy livestock, which is nearly always unavailable commercially, even from your county's rare breeds supplier. Opportunities must be looked for and seized. A lesson in doing just this can be learned from the story of Howard Keener of Northumberland who, after an exuberant evening at the Beresford Arms one Midsummer's Eve, took a torch from the village green's bonfire to light the path on his moonless walk home. He soon found himself approaching another light on the road, a faint

green glow, and realised that he was on the trail of a slowly moving herd of eerie fairy cattle. Although he was surprised to see the cows—each of them no larger than a child's toy—and their ghostly Lilliputian herdsman, the young Keener had enough sense to fall back a bit and follow them on their route to their fairy tump.

"It were like a hunnert lights was shining out that hillside," Keener later reported, describing the opened doorways to the herd's home beneath the mound. As the herdsman led the cattle through one of the lit portals, the brave Keener neatly wedged another open with a nearby stone. Pacing back to the herd's doorway, he stuck his smouldering torch in after them, then returned quickly to the held door. Keener stripped off his shirt to use as a net and was soon able to gather up seven of the miniature fairy cattle before fleeing the hill, itself belching smoke, the angry shouts of the spectral herdsman ringing in his ears.

A fit man, Keener outran the wrathful fairy and made it home with the tiny livestock, depositing them in a copper tub and pouring a ring of salt around it, thereby forming a mystic barrier over which no fey, be they herdsman or heifer, could cross. It was a trick he'd heard his grandmother mention. In the morning he was the proud owner of his own herd of fairy cattle and, using iron garden railing for fencing, built a small addition to his pasture for them. The descendants of the cows are there to this day for any who wish to visit them or to purchase a few, as I did years ago.

Whilst none of us can hope to be as lucky as Mr. Keener was on that fateful night, we can all prepare ourselves for a successful fairy cattle raid by bringing along a topped-up garden fumigator and a canvas sack to our nights at the pub, especially during the weeks of late spring and early summer, when fairy cattle are known to be on the move.

Although the washbasin-and-salt method will successfully keep fairy cattle happy overnight, the cows are creatures of the earth and should be moved to a pastoral setting as soon as possible. Do as Keener did and fence them in with iron flower bed railing, taking care to do it *adjacent to and not within* the fencing for your standard cattle. The fairy cow's build, whilst sturdy for its size, is no match for the misplaced or jealous hoof of even a smallish

Hereford. Start them in close-cropped grass, and they will keep their pasture tidy. In grass taller than a few inches, the fairy cattle have a tendency to become disoriented and overwhelmed, and such stress is unhealthy for them. A saucerful of water each morning is enough to keep a half dozen such cows sated and satisfied.

To prevent the loss of your cattle to the late-night counter-raid of an understandably cross fairy herdsman, all fairy cows, bulls, and calves must be secured inside appropriate shelter before sundown each day. Here, as in other aspects, is revealed the delicious thrift of Second-Sight smallholding. Does your village have a toy shop? The proprietor will be able to supply you with a doll's house version of a cattle barn at a significant savings compared to the cost of one for standard cattle. Explain to him your requirements — the size of your herd, the necessary height for interior stalls, the crucial need for walls and a roof which can keep out the elements and a barn door fitted with a stout lock. I've found that reasonable and scrupulous toymongers will sooner or later be able to find a fully accoutred barn for fairy cattle, although it can take some thorough description up front on the part of the Second-Sight small-holder. Once you've shown your dedication to fairy farming with the purchase of the barn, the toy merchant — full of inspiration at being co-conspirator in your success — will soon be calling you with suggestions for other little outbuildings and implements, not the other way round.

Just as the traditional farmer needs pay constant attention to his cows, the Second-Sight smallholder must care for his fairy cattle with daily minding. Milking is a delicate process and must be carried out in dawn's first silvery hour, before the herd commences its grazing. Happy is he who, lying prone in the mud before his converted doll's house, begins his day in service to himself and his kine, pinching tiny spurts of enchanted milk into miniature tin pails. I'm firm in my conviction that the only reason fairy cow's milk has yet to catch on as a national trend is that not enough people have tasted it. I find it brings a slight, not unwelcome walnut flavour to my tea, and when the spirit's got hold of me, I squirt some straight into my morning cuppa. And that's not all. I daresay I've got a few seelie cheeses in the works at the moment as well. Fingers crossed!

All farming is entered into with the end results in mind, and when it comes to cattle, one naturally thinks of beef. Fairy cattle have mercifully remained free from the taint of what is vulgarly known as "mad-cow disease," although anyone who imagines they can traipse cavalierly into the business of filling freezers with prime cuts of seelie beef will want to weigh the benefits and pitfalls of such an undertaking. It really is up to each Second-Sight smallholder to decide whether or not to go to the trouble of butchery and all it entails on such a small scale. I have tried my hand at it and found that although it is rewarding as an exercise in extracting full benefit and use from your fairy cattle, especially once they are too old to produce calves and milk, one doesn't get an awful lot of meat from each cow. Given the newer, more restrictive laws regarding livestock slaughter, the process is a do-it-yourself one, for better or worse. If you do decide to go through with it, I suggest you propose a summit involving yourself, the toy merchant, and the most sympathetic butcher you're able to find. Enquiries at local meat counters regarding such a project will, I've found, weed out any unfit candidates for the job. A successful bit of butchery in a tiny abattoir built by the toymonger will yield you and your allies a handful of the most mouth-watering beef you may ever taste, but the risk of finger lacerations is also quite high and the negative consequences of frustrated relations between the three of you must be taken into full account before you begin.

If there's one last thing I could encourage you to do apart from the activities outlined above, it would be to share some of your largesse with your neighbours and friends. Now that the word is out about the nutty milk from my "fairy dairy," as the villagers call it, I get no end of requests for the stuff. Be generous, and you shall see your generosity returned. The life of the Second-Sight smallholder isn't all rhubarb and roses, but on those cold mornings when the milk won't come, or in the black of night when your fairy calves are suffering from scours, forcing you to fuss about with microscopic rehydration treatments by lamplight whilst covered in infectious muck, it's worth reminding yourself that we're all in this together.

A FEW WORDS
ABOUT
FLOWER-FAIRIES

*The Flower-Fairy a Deceiver • Its
Usefulness • Children • Stalking Flower-Fairies •
A Golden Afternoon • Absinthe and
Second Sight • Three Cautions • Successful
Integration • Village Fairs*

ONCE, THE REALM OF FAERIE was interwoven with every aspect of life for all people, young and old alike. Today, however, the Fairy Kingdom is associated mainly with the world of childhood. This shift has been the result of calculated efforts by the flower-fairies, known to everyone by their benign depictions in children's storybooks, each one of them paired with a particular blooming flower or fruit tree.

Whilst seldom seen, the scheming flower-fairies are regular whisperers into the ears of poets and painters. Their mutterings are invariably meant to engender benevolent sympathy from mankind, and in this regard the flower-fairies have acted as unsurpassed public-relations agents for the Fairy Kingdom. Over the past few centuries their infiltration of the storytelling medium — in picture books, popular imagery, and film — has resulted in the all-pervasive conception of the overwhelming majority of Fairyland's inhabitants as sweet, endearing, and useful only when it comes to teaching this or that moral in a child's bedtime fable.

Precious few concepts could be further from the truth. One realises, upon reflection, that the flower-fairies' keen focus upon this image campaign is self-serving not only to the fey as an entire race but to the flower-fairies in particular, as they have proven to be a devilishly useful participant in the works of the modern fruit and vegetable gardener.

Schoolchildren and their nannies may protest, but the fact remains that the flower-fairies' numbers thrive under managed conservation and their presence and industry lend undreamt-of fertility; fuller, better-tasting fruit; and heightened health and productivity levels to the gardens, orchards, and greenhouses into which they are integrated. Anyone who desires these qualities and outcomes in their own horticultural endeavours has but to obtain a handful of flower-fairies of their own and, with a few easy-to-master practices, incorporate the twittering sprites into the works.

When we are young, we can see flower-fairies easily, but as we age, there is something which occludes these frisky sprites from our view. Scientific explanations vary, but it is my own opinion that in the act of growing to adulthood we tire of the mindless frolics of the pear-blossom chatterer and its kin. This fading away of the flower-fairies would be without drawback were these gossamer-winged gossipers not so damned useful to the practical botanist. For in spite of their caperings or perhaps as a strange side effect of them, each and every blossom in the garden plot perks up in the presence of flower-fairies.

For children, the prospect is an easy one. The flower-fairies are there, plain as day, flitting from blossom to blossom and emitting high-pitched squeaks. And if they can be seen, they can be caught. Among these young people, the work is all of a quick pass of the hand and a depositing into a glass jar. But let us address the botanist who has grown past childhood, the one for whom flower-fairies are not so much storybook characters come to life as they are key elements to growing prize-winning aubergines. To this eager gardener, one who wishes to see the fairies but is unable, my message is a short, sure one: Despair not! In fact, rejoice! Rejoice in the freedom of not having your every step compromised by the scuttlings of spriggans, the air you breathe alive with imps, the potting shed sinks clogged with nixies. All these gardening bugbears are still present, mind you, but prove less of a nuisance whilst invisible. Unfortunately, before one may reap the benefits of a fully stocked flower-fairy garden, one must be able to *see* the creatures. The Second Sight is not a blessing, though. In my storied history, I've found it to be more of a curse. But as much as it pains me to instruct readers in the ways and means of bringing on the Second Sight, even if it be temporary, the fruits, as it were, of such labours are a fair prize for any momentary suffering.

The first step in embarking on a flower-fairy gathering expedition is to determine where best to find a prolific swarm. One could, of course, follow the local children on their afternoon scampers, having the youngsters point out which clumps of daisies would yield the most flower-fairies if pounced upon with, say, a butterfly net one happened to be carrying for such an occasion. But children can be a fickle lot, prone to trickery if they believe they have the chance to witness a respectable grown man make a fool of himself. One need look no further than the case of devoted fairy hunter Sir Arthur Conan Doyle and assorted members of the Theosophy Society in the 1920 Cottingley Beck incident for an example of such a duping. No, if one truly desires to gather a decent assortment of flower-fairies, one is best served by going it alone, especially if one hopes to come out not only with a garden bursting with unsurpassed fruit but also with one's dignity intact.

Look for lush patches of flowers or fruit blossoms you wish to cultivate successfully in your

own garden, and set up your operation there. If this happens to put you in one of the wild places of the countryside, then so much the better, for your work will, under the best of circumstances, require several hours of uninterrupted concentration. For the purposes of this example we will talk about strawberries, but these techniques can be adapted easily for any flowering plant, even fruit trees.

If your most fecund plot of longed-for vegetation exists within the boundaries of a fellow gardener's estate, do your best to curry favour with him, perhaps offering exchange of goods from your own smallholding in return for a chance at taking home some of his flower-fairies. I've found that most gardeners, following an initial period of apprehension, see a reasonable trade when it is presented to them. In fact, a transaction such as this—my fruits for their fairies—has been described to me by more than one of my neighbours as *more than reasonable*. Try not to let on that you're getting the far better end of the bargain.

The needed articles of equipment for a proper flower-fairy hunt are few. To the aforementioned butterfly net and appropriate bed of flowers, one need but make two additions. A dozen canning jars with tight lids is the first. The second is a bottle of top-quality absinthe, along with a field kit of absinthe glass, sugar lumps, a pitcher of ice water, and the absinthe drinker's trademark silver spoon. Prepare each jar by pouring into it a quarter-inch of absinthe and dropping in a freshly plucked straw-berry blossom, replacing the lids so as to avoid spilling the contents.

A Golden Afternoon

That period of hazy, idle time between luncheon and afternoon tea is best for fairy-snatching, I've found. Locate a comfortable bit of earth on which to sit, a lush patch of strawberries in full bloom before you, their blossoms within easy reach. All your accoutrements — net, jars, absinthe bottle, and trappings — must be arranged behind you.

Like gardening itself, the process takes time, concentration, and patience. Unlike gardening, however, in the work of flower-fairy stalking one is not cultivating flowers but rather a simple veneer of trust. What you hope to achieve during the course of the next few hours is an affinity betwixt yourself and Nature, a bond of confidence between your personality and those of the flitting, buzzing sprites floating as-yet-invisible above the blooms. And this trust, this *rapport*, is established between man and fairy in much the same manner as it is fixed between friends and strangers alike — with potent alcohol.

The Second-Sight applications of absinthe drinking are as vast and time-honoured as the literature on this elixir. "The first stage is like ordinary drink-

goblinproofing one's chicken coop

ing, the second when you begin to see monstrous and cruel things," said the diligent absinthe devotee Oscar Wilde. "But if you can persevere, you will enter in upon the third stage where you see things that you want to see." And the French painter Henri de Toulouse-Lautrec, whilst decadent in several areas of his life and work, was spot on in his study of the Second Sight, bringing on regular, voluntary visions of *la fée verte* through dedicated application of absinthe.

We must follow in the footsteps of these pioneering seers.

Reach back for the absinthe bottle, pop out the cork, and slosh a quick drop of it here and there amidst the strawberries. Flower-fairies are powerless to resist the scent of this French spirit. While you're at it, prepare and consume a quick dash of the stuff yourself.

As with many interactions with the Fairy Kingdom, subtlety in this endeavour is overrated. Drink as much absinthe as you need and be sure to keep freshening up your sprinklings of it round the strawberry patch. The fourth glass usually does the trick for me, but unseasoned "goodpeople gardeners"—or those mercifully untouched by a natural inclination towards the Second Sight—may require further quaffs.

If the initial wormwood-tinged afternoon spent sitting in the strawberry patch—absinthe bottle artfully hidden behind your back and butterfly net close at hand—is not enough to ensnare seven or eight flower-fairies, you may not be trying hard enough. Calm your agitated mind. Stare at the blossoms. Have another drink. Repeat your mantra: "They will come . . . they will come . . . they will come . . ." Say it quietly but confidently. Assure yourself of it. And as the elixir begins to take full effect, do your best to keep from listing. This will only unnerve the fairies and also carries the risk of satisfying any busybody neighbours watching you, intent on cracking the code to your gardening prowess.

Success may be had after one such afternoon or several. Try not to wait more than a few days between sessions, as the blooming season is nearly as ephemeral as the sought-after blossom-haunters themselves.

Eventually, if you have followed these instructions diligently, victory will be yours. As the outline of every other thing around you begins to blur, the air as murky as the fluid in your seventh glass of absinthe, new forms begin to clarify before you. *The first of your flower-fairies is now within your reach.* You could be forgiven for mistaking the fairy for an insect or a flash of sunlight, but the careful observer will notice how, as the creature nears each blossom, it takes on a corporeal form to the extent that one may make out a face or even a bit of glamour meant to resemble clothing.

When this moment occurs, three points must be kept firmly in mind if the goodpeople gardener is to emerge triumphant:

1. *Do not listen to the fairy's speech.* The flower-fairy may employ its instinctual defence and attempt to reason with you. If you engage in such a conversation, you will be opening yourself to the creature's terrible powers of moral persuasion. This ability is the basis for any number of children's stories, and whilst the advice squeaked by a flower-fairy may seem trite and

overly simple between the covers of an edition of the collected works of Hans Christian Andersen, when one is sitting in the hot afternoon sun reeling from the effects of seven or eight glasses of strong drink, one is incredibly susceptible to the fairy's preaching. The flower-fairies are accomplished orators, employing smarm and their own twisted brand of maudlin "logic" to convince listeners of the most outlandish things, all of which are in service to regaining their freedom. Watch for it. Nip it, if you'll pardon the expression, squarely in the bud. If the fairy begins to speak, simply begin humming a tuneless song as you tighten your fingers round the handle of your butterfly net. Success is all but within your literal grasp. This is no time to falter.

2. *Avoid lunging.* The fairy will likely flit about the blossom for a moment, no longer than three or four seconds. It may then descend closer to the ground in order to inspect the soil wet with absinthe. This will give you additional time, however fleeting, in which to position the net over the fairy. It will sense your doing so but

as it attempts to fly upwards will find its trajectory blocked by the net, now brought down upon it, and will be well and truly caught.

3. *Remain sensible.* Once the flower-fairy is in your net, transfer it gingerly to one of the canning jars and twist the lid on tightly. Do not fall a sentimental victim to the fairy's melodramatic flailings or by any of its apings of the international gesture for choking. If you do, you run the risk of repeating the mistake, passed down erroneously through generations of would-be goodpeople gardeners, of ventilating the lid of the jar with "air holes." The fairy is fine. It needs no air to survive. Nor does it feed on the thoughts and actions of well-behaved children, despite what your governess may have told you. The flower-fairy is a creature of sunlight and reverie and, as such, the ideal environment for it, at least for the time being, is securely within a sealed jar containing a single plucked blossom and a modicum of absinthe.

Once you've popped a fairy into each of your jars, you may declare the day an unqualified success. Rise to your feet slowly, transfer your vessels to a sunlit window, and have a nap to sleep off the lingering effects of the absinthe or any of the flower-fairies' last-ditch entreaties for a peaceful release. They will be fine in the jars for up to a week, but I daresay you won't be able to wait that long before you get on with integrating them into your veg patch.

The novice goodpeople gardener will be pleased to discover that the grafting of flower-fairies is not that different from the standard traditional practice. After a day or two on the shelf, the half-pickled fairies will be thoroughly calmed and will come along easily. Unscrew the lid to the jar, and with a gentle

goblinproofing one's chicken coop

hand pluck out each docile sprite as you need it, laying the fairy on a clean handkerchief. Refer to past issues of *The Journal of the Royal Horticultural Society* for grafting guidance, finding stems (in the case of herbaceous bushes) and twigs (when grafting to fruit trees) of about the same girth as the fairy's leg. Remember to make the cut *only to the plant, not to the fairy*. The plant itself has enough strength to recover from such an incision; your flower-fairy has not. A close wrapping of nurserymen's tape is all that's needed to secure the two together.

The true beauty of the fully realised goodpeople garden is that, beyond these simple provisions, there is no need to arrange any further measures against the fairy's attempts to escape, for it will make none. In its flitterings before, the flower-fairy has wanted nothing but union with its counterpart in the vegetable kingdom, and now you have provided it. To the extent that these calculating creatures can experience emotion, one could say that the newly integrated fairy, its leg soundly fixed to its beloved plant, is happy. It will live out the rest of its life in a state of idyllic conjunction, and in doing so will provide unprecedented bounty to its plant and the others nearby. As these vitalising effects last but one season, at harvest time the strawberry-blossom fairies can be turned over with the compost and the apple-tree sprites snapped off and given to the neighbourhood children to arrange with their dolls and toys.

A final consideration the goodpeople gardener is bound to make is whether to enter these devilishly good fruits into the village fairs and other competitions. Personally, I'm all for it. It is only a matter of time before the work of integrating fairies into one's garden and orchard becomes standard practice, and it is difficult to conceive of a better rallying banner for the movement than a garland of blue ribbons earned thusly hanging in the window of one's potting shed.

THE ABUSES OF ENCHANTMENT

The Country of Love • Angling in Cornwall • A Pleasantly Unsettling Meeting • Harmony • Trouble and Strife • The Levee Breaks • A Peculiar Visitor • Bewilderment and Angling

WHILST NOT FALLING SQUARELY within the boundaries of the Fairy Kingdom, the borders of the mist-enshrouded country of Love do overlap it here and there, so I think this as good a place as any to warn young persons as to its similar dangers. I was in love once, and the effect was as disorienting and full of contradiction as many a Faerie encounter.

I happened, one afternoon in the spring, to be angling alone off the coast of Zennor, in Cornwall. The inlets around the rocky cliffs attract a particularly abundant crowd of mackerel and conger there at that time of year, and I had never failed in bringing home a creel brimming with succulent denizens of the deep. But fate and the tide must have conspired against me that day, for the only thing I caught that afternoon was verse after verse of a lonesome-sounding sea-song drifting in on the breeze from just to the south of where I stood. Not usually one for ditties, unless they be of the merrymaking sort sung down at the pub, I ignored the tune for what must have been hours.

I take it back. There was one other object I'd caught. My basket was no more full than it had been when I'd arrived save for a singularly strange object, a pearl-and barnacle-encrusted comb which had become tangled in my line early on in the session. No use trying to eat *that*, I thought, but it was pretty, in a way, so I saved it on the off chance it and my hard-luck story might be traded for a drink that night at the Tinners Arms.

Dejected, I turned and began slumping back to the car when my pace was halted by a most extraordinary sight. There on the rocks, in the direction from which I'd heard the song, sat a young woman. She appeared to be enjoying the beachside's charms *au naturel*, and her impressively long hair was unbraided and artfully arranged, just barely descandalising her lean form. Her posture was flawless, and I admired the way the day's fading light seemed to make her alabaster skin glow.

Perhaps I admired it a moment too long, for as our eyes met she lowered her head slightly, keeping her gaze stuck to mine, her shoulders broadening beneath her plaits as she took in a lungful of the cool sea air. The atmosphere between us thickened measurably.

I opened the conversation. It was only polite.

"Oh, hello, what? Was that you singing all this time?"

She spoke, her voice possessing a crispness unlike anything I'd ever heard, save the peerless breaking of the surface of this beach's same waters by a majestic blue shark I'd hooked there, circa 1972.

"Are you a man?"

My initial reaction, as so often it is, was one of incredulity. *Am I a man?* What sort of question is that? Why, take a look, I felt like saying. Here I am, head up top, feet beneath, all the appropriate pieces and accessories between. Am I a man, indeed! But then, perhaps an effect of the intake of too much sea air, I felt something soften inside of me near the region of the solar plexus, and I realised there were two possible reasons for this innocent young lady's question. Either she may have struck her delicate head upon one of the rocks and was just now regaining her bearings, or she might be demurely asking a different sort of question altogether.

Of course. Of course!

"Y-yes," I stammered, still a tad dazed by the aforementioned interior softening. I had completely forgotten my manners. "Here, take my coat. You must be freezing." She accepted the proffered jacket, a smart tweed three-quarter length number with an understated check pattern, and whilst the fit was a bit large on her, there was something to the resulting look which engendered yet more sensations in my midsection. Most strange it was. Something akin to nausea, I suppose one could say, but in a pleasing sort of way.

"If you are a man, then we are now married," this rather forward creature said, taking my hand and standing and catching me quite by surprise.

"Oh, don't be silly," I protested. "But do come along and let's get you somewhere warmer and drier." As I led her to the car, she began to sing again, a jollier tune this time and one which seemed to go straight to work on my gizzards, picking up where the softening was happening and giving me no end of novel and molten sensation. I drove the few miles to the cottage where I lived in those days in a sort of trance, scarcely aware of anything but the mellifluous song.

I shan't go into any detail whatsoever here, but by morning there could be no doubt as to the question of whether the young woman—she said her name was Cordelia—and I were man and wife. And a pleasant pair we were. All I had in the kitchen was a tin of kippers and some bread I toasted, but she devoured the breakfast with surprising zeal. Cordelia told me she came from the village of Tidewall, a hamlet to the north prone to flooding, from what I could gather. Her parents were fallen aristocrats. I'd never heard of the place or the family, despite being thoroughly familiar with that bit of coastline, but thought it rude to do anything but nod and smile. Poor thing, I thought, she really must have struck her head. No contusion was visible, however, and whatever the impact may have done to her profile, I had to admit that the effect was stunning.

We spent the next several weeks in a state of unalloyed bliss. Cordelia sewed herself dresses from silk and decorated them with shells, glass beads, and any other seaside trinkets she found about the cottage. She had a hard time in the kitchen, especially with the stove, but happily cleaned the house and ate fish and greens by the bushel-basket, singing between bites. Cordelia was a sweet one, to be sure, though a bit peculiar. Each time I held her hand, I found a few grains of sand between her fingers, and one merry afternoon as I gave her a foot rub, I bit my tongue to keep from remarking on the slight webbing I found between her toes. But she was beautiful, and for the first time in my life, I could say I was a man who knew the touch of romantic love. I longed to express my feelings and did so with a stream of gifts — new dresses

she wore happily and jewellery which pleased her, especially pearls. Shoes were another matter. Cordelia rarely wore them, and only sandals when she did. What she did ask for over and over were things for her hair. She adored dressing it with baubles and even took to sporting the occasional tiara, which was amusing to me at first, if a bit eccentric. And the outfits she would wear on our evenings out! Her dresses she sometimes would re-sew into the most ingenious layered arrangements which, whilst still pretty, were fit more for a stage production than for walking along the town's main street. The village children sometimes followed us home with jeers of "Mister and Missus Princess" and tips of the hat to "Her Royal Shoeless." Cordelia just smiled and tightened her grip on my arm each time I hinted at raising my walking stick against the blighters. Her hair was as long and luxuriant as when we met, and she attended to it with a procession of combs I brought home for her. She seized each one hungrily from me, running it through her flowing hair and singing as she did so. But the song was invariably a sombre one, and after no more than two or three sessions with each comb, she set

goblinproofing one's chicken coop

it aside in a seldom-used dresser drawer. "It's not the right one," I overheard her say as she assigned what I thought a particularly pretty silver comb to the drawer one evening in late summer.

I won't fool you by saying this business with the combs was the sole chink in the armour of our love. I ceased trying with the romantic poetry early on after eliciting naught more than a wan smile from Cordelia. Her constant singing was festive when she would burst out with sailors' tunes, and the stories she told me of how she first heard them were exciting, but sometimes raised the hackles of what can only be called my unfairly jealous heart.

Our arguments were often rooted in what I saw as reluctance on her part to share morsels of her exceptionally odd background with me. She told me she came from a large family and that her childhood was one of singing games and lessons in swimming and fishing. She said something about being part of a school, which sounded like one of those experimental programmes dreamed up by "progressive" parents not interested in a proper education for the youth. Fishing, swimming, singing . . . "Age of Aquarius," indeed!

All the same, we settled into a mostly happy companionship, travelling in the autumn to Sennen Cove, near Land's End, where we had dinner with Cordelia's sister Marina and her husband Steve, a semi-retired tugboat captain. They had been blessed with a lawless mob of children, all of them cheerful enough, even if they did get a bit short of breath after capering about for very long. The green tinge to each of their complexions was something I decided was not worth mentioning.

After what may have been justly called the one too many glasses of whisky Steve and I shared that evening, punctuated by his increasingly bawdy revelations regarding his and Marina's love life — with an odd wink at me accompanying each detail — Cordelia and I graciously begged off for the night.

The evening was innocuous enough, but as a grain of sand doesn't always catch just so in an oyster to produce a pearl but rather sometimes goes straight for the eye of the otherwise perfectly contented swimmer, so that conversation lodged itself between Cordelia and your narrator, causing a minor but regular irritation.

When the New Year rolled around and we'd been cooped up in the house for far too long that winter, I was struck, as happens to me that time of year, with the urge to wander to new places, to see landscapes and meet people I might otherwise never encounter. And this time, I thought, I can bring my lady love, my shoreline bride, my Cordelia.

"I say, darling," I said, "Why don't we knock off to this Tidewall village of yours, get some fresh air, and drop in on your mum and dad? You must miss them terribly, as I'm sure they do you. It's been almost a year, and you haven't been back." At this, the fragile Cordelia erupted into tears. She sobbed uncontrollably, and no amount of ministrations of tea and repetitions of "there, there" was enough to console her. She had been sitting doing some needle-point work—a pirate ship theme, I believe—and the flood of her great salty tears was fierce enough not only to drip from the canvas she held in her hands but also to downgrade my first edition of W.D.M. Bell's *The Wanderings of an Elephant Hunter* which I'd left on the small table next to her chair. It had been a "very fine," but now . . .

When Cordelia did gain hold of herself sufficiently that I thought she might be able to hear my voice, I ventured a careful enquiry.

"What is it, my pet? I didn't mean to upset you."

"I feel as though you don't know who I really am!" she bawled, her watery delivery carrying with it an exasperated spite which stung me as though I'd got hold of the business end of a jellyfish who, after long chase, yet retained a final jolt of electricity in its arsenal.

"And how should I?" I retorted, perhaps a bit harshly. "You never truly open up to me about anything. We never go to your village. Here we are, married for nearly a year, and I've never even met your parents. It's as though you hide from me all I could ever hope to find out about you."

"You, sir, are denser than an oyster shell!" Cordelia spat.

I'm not known at the club as the man to go to for instructions in holding one's temper, but this trait is thankfully balanced by the good sense to know when the train of conversation has departed the rails altogether and is heading for the cliff. Some fresh air was indeed in order, but perhaps best taken alone. I set down my tea cup, rose from my armchair, and walked to the closet near the front hall, where I had stashed my fishing kit the springtime previous.

"I'll return when both our tempers have cooled somewhat," I announced, rummaging about for this and that piece of necessary equipment. The last object I pulled from the closet was my creel, and as I did, something rattled against its wicker wall. Unfastening the top, I reached in and snatched hold of the pale, barnacle-encrusted comb I'd caught on that fateful day nearly a year before.

"There," I said, tossing the comb onto the seat of the hall tree. "Perhaps that comb will do for you what all those others could not." I was scarcely about to wait for a reply from Cordelia, but on my way out the front door, I did catch sight of her face and noticed that she was gazing covetously at the comb and that her countenance had brightened considerably.

Maybe I had been too rash, for when I returned from shore — again without catching a single fish — Cordelia was nowhere to be found. The comb was gone, and apart from her and the clothes she'd been wearing, it was all that was missing from the house. She didn't return that night or the next, and I grew concerned for her. A call to her sister's proved fruitless. Marina and Steve seemed concerned, she less so than he, who just repeated his condolences for my ill luck. "Just be happy you've had the experience, mate," he intoned as I hung up. And for the only time in my life, I felt a bit sorry for myself as well. Perhaps I *had* been too rash. But damn it all, who *was* that woman, anyway?

I never did see Cordelia again. The closest thing I got to a goodbye came on the anniversary of our meeting, when there was a knock at the cottage door. Opening it, I found myself face-to-face with a most extraordinary man. His lips were full, protruding, and a touch blue, and his eyes were wide-set in his hairless head. His strangely tailored suit positively dripped with, what was it, sweat?

"I represent the solicitors Gillman, Seasbury, and Codd. These documents are for your inspection," gurgled the damp fellow, pressing a sheaf of soggy paperwork into my hands.

It would only be putting off the inevitable not to read and sign the divorce petition, so I did so straight away, noting that this bizarre fellow's law firm was located in Tidewall, Cordelia's old home. At least she'd made it back to her people. The thought gave me some small measure of comfort as I handed the papers to the moist solicitor, who burbled what must have been an acknowledgement before turning and flapping off in a westerly direction.

I've remained a confirmed bachelor ever since the incident. The ways of love are perhaps an ill fit for my personality. I did bump into Steve a few years later, during an unrelated visit to Sennen Cove, and bought him a pint at the Old Success. He told me that he and Marina hadn't seen Cordelia, but that they had caught word that she'd taken up with a young marine biologist in Newquay, some miles north of where she and I first met. Ah well. We drank to their happiness.

Aside from the occasional reverie of bewilderment concerning romance and its trappings, episodes of which have happily tapered off as the years roll by, all that's changed in my life since my early bachelor years is my prowess with my angling. I just can't seem to catch a fish, ever. It's the strangest thing, and I assure you that despite consulting all the manuals and periodicals on the subject, I haven't the foggiest notion as to why it is so.

The Fight Afield

FIRST AID FOR THE FAIRY-SHOT

The Dangers of Going Out of Doors • Hostage No More • Cautions, Countermeasures, Cures • Elf-Song • Fairy Food and Drink • Dancing • Elf-Shot • A Lonely Path

ANY PERSON VENTURING outside the wainscoted confines of their own home, let alone beyond the bounds of their village, is entering a veritable wilderness in which the fey, not men, can unfortunately be said to have the advantage. Here, any semblance of a life without the potential for sudden abduction or unprovoked violence is but a gross illusion—at best a lull in the ongoing struggle between humanity and our immortal adversary, at worst a pernicious duping of the senses brought about by wicked fairy magic.

Perverse to a fault, fey attacks are deviously cloaked under the guise of countryside situations one might deem charming, although the word takes on new definition when one pauses to consider the grisly results of being "charmed" away to a lifetime of imprisonment in Fairyland. The key to your well-being lies in your peering past this disguise, in your seeing such tricks and traps for what they really are.

Unsurprisingly, given the popular misconceptions of Faerie, it is often said that such attacks are carried out to keep mankind from penetrating too deeply into fairy country, sometimes poetically referred to as "the last of the wild spaces." Whilst I am a sworn protector of the natural splendour of the countryside, I draw the line at being held psychological hostage by territorial elves and their addle-pated human supporters. It is with this conviction that I implore you not to be swayed by fear, but to go bravely into field and forest prepared to face the realities of fairy assault.

And here I impart good news to the intrepid souls wishing to emerge from the shadow of possible abduction or attack. There are many dangers, indeed, but all of them are avoidable should one spend a bit

the fight afield

of time preparing for their eventuality. Furthermore, these precautions utilise objects familiar to us all and tactics rewarded by a bit of practice at home.

My own brand of "fairy field medicine," if you will, is organised around a trio of easy-to-recall principles. These are *Cautions*, *Countermeasures*, and *Cures*. As the names imply, the Cautions are preparations of knowledge and equipment; the Countermeasures, actions to be undertaken to address fairy attacks in progress; and the Cures, remedial procedures to enact should prevention prove impossible.

What follows is a listing of examples of the principal forms of fairy attack and which of the "three Cs" is most effective in each case.

Elf-Song

All of us have, at some point during a walk outside, paused to listen to melodious birdsong. Did you know that this simple pleasure is one which fairies regularly exploit in order to turn unsuspecting young members of society into withered husks of women and men? For the song one hears is just as likely to be an unseelie lullaby as it is an innocent songbird's warble.

Every British child has heard the story of Shon ap Shenkin, a tale similar in many ways to Rip Van Winkle's in America: A good-natured country person rests beneath a tree where he is lulled to sleep by fairies, in Shon's case by charming elf-song. What seems like a nodding off of but a few minutes is in fact a slumber lasting decades. The victim awakes only to crumble to dust in short order or, as was the situation with Van Winkle, to become a walking curiosity in one's own village.

Neither of these grim fates will befall me, however, because I never leave the house without a standard bell-alarm clock packed among the objects in my day-hike kit. This I procure from my satchel and set for half an hour each and every time I find myself settling down against the base of a tree to enjoy a particularly soothing snippet of birdsong, on the not unlikely chance the tune is actually sleep-inducing fairy music. It is the simplest of Cautions, and I daresay it's saved my life more than once. I've tried compact "travel" alarm clocks and found them less satisfying than the classic bedside style. You might think it an unnecessary burden to pack one with you on your walks. You may feel self-conscious the first few times you wind your alarm clock and set it in your lap. Perhaps you think the ticking of the hands or the ringing of the bell upsets the pristine perfection of the wild. But if the OED were ever to include an illustration alongside its entry for "mortification," it would be one of the unthinking fool who forgot to set an alarm clock upon first hearing elf-song, only to wake up a century later and turn to dust on his great-grandnephew's doorstep.

Once the bell sounds, frightening off any warbling Faerie tricksters, I always like to bring myself back to full consciousness with a set of isometric stretches against the tree, followed by three loud recitations of my grocery list, which I am never without.

Think! It's all I ask of you.

Fairy Food and Drink

Once you've got the proper mindset regarding the Cautions, it is but child's play to recognise other anti-fey preparations. Fairy food and drink are notorious for trapping the unwitting in Fairyland, if not simply poisoning them. Won't you feel smart then, the next time a band of shrivelled goblin merchants attempts to harm you in such a way, even if to the untrained observer it appears merely that roadside fruit vendors are offering you a small sample of their hard-earned produce? For at that moment will you extract a hearty sandwich from your daypack, biting into it secure in the knowledge that you will not be whisked away to their horrid underground grotto. No, the only danger you'll face on that day

is potential choking due to smug laughter whilst keenly devouring your sandwich. Don't be swayed by the looks of affronted confusion plastered across the goblins' faces, or by their mutterings of "Well, I never. . . ." These are but pathetic, last-ditch efforts to get you to taste of their fruit, a single bite of which will deliver you straight into their clutches. Three cheers for the Cautions!

Dancing

A May Day festival or other village celebration is a fine time for dancing, and there's no reason not to throw prudence to the wind during the merrymaking, save one: the risk of fairy abduction. Should there be a fey fiddler secreted among the musicians, or a seelie stepper on the dance floor, then the final tune of the evening could end with you dancing off with them, never to return. Thus, on an evening when you find yourself about to dance with a fine-looking stranger at the close of the night's festivities, I encourage you to do as I do. First, pull from your pocket a generous ball of string, tying the end of it round your left index finger. Then hand the rest of the string to the parish priest, himself immune to fairy magic and a person with your soul's salvation foremost in his heart. Now you may turn to your ravishing partner and reel away to your heart's content. Rest assured you won't be going home with *that* treacherous vixen tonight, my friend! I've used this tactic a number of times, and the very fact that I'm able to teach it to you now is testament to its efficacy.

As a corollary, remember that *any* villager dancing the night away with a gorgeous stranger is a likely mark for fairy abduction. If they've not sensibly enacted the "String Caution" described above, they may yet be saved by a Countermeasure in the form of a well-timed tackle from behind. I've found in my experience that hardly anyone *enjoys* such a rescue, but I'm able to sleep at night knowing I've done the right thing.

Even if a misunderstanding over the intent of your humanitarian intervention has barred you from attending this season's festival, you may still find a way to enact helpful Countermeasures for others. Walk the paths of the nearby forests, your watchful eyes on the lookout for "fairy rings," that is, circular arrangements of any variety of mushroom growing in the wild. These rings are the dancing grounds of the fairies, and anyone crossing into them is liable to be trapped in the Fairy Kingdom. What is it to you, giving up an afternoon to sit near the fairy ring cautioning other hikers from stepping into the

snare? Should they not hear you, or perhaps not grasp the seriousness of crossing this mystical mycological boundary, it's not out of the question to employ a dash of *jiu-jitsu* to veer them round it. It's more difficult than one might expect, this manoeuvre, especially if you're trying to avoid stepping into the circle yourself.

Elf-Shot

The widespread prevalence of fairy assaults means it is sadly impossible for us to stop them all, no matter how hard we try. This is doubly true when it comes to attacks at the green-knuckled hands of fairy archers firing a peculiar ammunition known as "elf-shot" at men and livestock alike.

Appearing in the aftermath as one or more flint arrowheads strewn about in the grass, elf-shot is in fact invisible during its deployment, leaving no mark or cut to show its entry into the victim. Let not elf-shot's ephemeral nature deceive you as to its potency, for it is responsible for countless cases of rheumatism, slurred speech, muddled senses, impaired memory, and loss of command over one's own face and limbs.

The only solace we may find in this deplorable state of affairs is that the remedy to these various ills is to be found in the elf-shot itself. Folk wisdom has long held that any cow fallen victim to fairy archers may be healed of its infirmities by making the animal drink from a trough into which an elf-shot arrowhead has been dropped. A moment's thought is more than sufficient to translate this remedy into a Cure which may benefit our fellow man. A flint

arrowhead dropped into the evening pint of a person you suspect may be the victim of elf-shot produces, from the evidence I've gathered, startlingly quick and undeniable results. Those thought of as intellectually slow begin to spout full paragraphs straightaway, and the lame walk, if not run. Of course, reports of these miracle cures always reach my ears second-hand, as I make it a point to depart the pub immediately after slipping the elf-shot into the various pint glasses. After all, I'm not so vain as to need to reap the glory from such a simple act. I implore you to exhibit similar modesty when effecting Cures.

The lack of public knowledge concerning the Cautions, Countermeasures, and Cures is a continual source of surprise to me. Despite their being among the oldest forms of field medicine, these antifey tactics seem to be less understood, and consequently less appreciated, with each passing year. The path of the paranormal paramedic is often a lonely, thankless one; truly it is. Reassure yourself that what you are doing is for the good of humanity, and trust that you will find people sympathetic to your calling. As a lover of the countryside and its countless charms, I wish not only that you too can increase your enjoyment of these pleasures, but also that you gain a reputation among the rural populace as a stalwart defender of their way of life.

ON GNOMING

*Springtime Means Gnoming • Proper Outfitting •
The Hunting Party • Indications of Gnome Life •
A Technique for Riflemen • Trickery •
Cookery • The Trouble of Trolls*

THE COMING OF SPRING means many things to many people, but to me its principal message is this—time for gnoming! Crafty and fast, gnomes are one of the season's most rewarding catches.

Although the gnomish population has dropped slightly in recent years, seasoned hunters should take this not as a deterrent to bagging gnomes but rather as an incentive. Gnomes are more of a nuisance than a help to the people of the countryside. They befriend woodland creatures and invite them into the field and garden to eat freely of the farmer's bounty. Their latticework of burrows undermines the integrity of the forest floor, creating nasty traps for the hoof of the horse or the foot of the heavy brother-in-law. But if anyone needs an ultimate rationale for taking up arms against these diminutive devils, I urge them to consider the wonderfully dark, earthy taste of gnomish meat. A dish combining mushrooms, fresh-picked vegetables, and gnome is surely one of springtime's greatest pleasures.

The intelligent gnomer should outfit himself with the proper equipment. Stealth is essential when tracking gnomes, so make your first priority the sourcing of a quiet pair of thin-soled stalking boots. Gnomes

goblinproofing one's chicken coop

gravitate towards temperate climates and wooded habitats, shunning swamps, so you needn't bother with those hip waders. Wear drab-coloured clothing in keeping with the terrain on which you will be hunting. Dull browns and greens usually do the trick.

Choose your weapon carefully. Because your quarry stands no taller than one cubit when full grown, it's easy to overestimate the required firepower. This can be a grave mistake, resulting in your bringing along an implement which will blast this tasty fairy into so much pixie dust. It's better to first ask yourself, "What *sort* of gnomer am I?" Should you think yourself a cunning stalker, you may best be served by carrying a powerful slingshot. The patient archer is paired nicely with a precise cross-bow. For those quick brutes among the gnoming set, a potent club gets the job done. Rifles are categorically out of the question for beginners, but as I will explain later, a skilled marksman can bag a gnome with a rifle without even piercing the delectable creature's skin. A final essential bit of equipment is the elephant gun, for reasons that will be explored at the close of this essay.

Gnoming parties are best limited to two, or to one hunter and a reliable hound. Station yourself near the entrance to a gnome's house, which you will discern entwined in the spreading roots of a large oak tree. Look for shrunken examples of furniture recalling the Arts and Crafts Movement littering the front garden. Dawn and dusk are the preferred hours for your grim vigil, as it is just before sunrise that the gnome leaves his house to go to the woodshop and nightfall when he returns.

Gnomes have an olfactory sense nearly as sharp as their joining skill, so the successful gnomer will take care to smear his skin and clothing with generous amounts of *les odeurs de la forêt*, as the French would have it. Mix elderberries, broken-up toadstools, and stag droppings to make a thick paste, rubbing it on yourself and any weapons you have brought. This will optimise your chance of evading the gnome's keen nostrils.

When day and night are at their inbetweenest, that is when you, the wisest gnomer of the wood, smeared in elderberry paste and sling at the ready, will observe the telltale sign of the gnome as he saunters down his forest path. That sign is none other than the gnome's conical red hat. Each gnome wears this distinctive headgear in all periods of wakefulness and sleep. It is that selfsame cap that will prove to be our antagonist's undoing, for it shines like a crimson beacon atop his head.

A well-placed stone or crossbow bolt, or some deft cudgel work, will knock the life out of any healthy gnome. Take care to aim for the creature's head, and hit hard. The gnome's cranium is thick and, centuries ago, inspired the now-popular term "gnomeskull" to indicate a person of slow wits.

The rifle-wielding sharpshooter must take a different approach, because any bullet which hits a gnome will take more gnome than not. What's the use spending all your time smearing stag fewmets if all you've got to show for your trouble is a mangled pulp of a fairy that might offer up as much sustenance as a malnourished stoat? No, the marksman's technique is subtle, sporting, and offers more options for the successful gnomer. It is known as the "concussion shot" and, in my opinion, is the only way to hunt gnomes.

The trickiest bit about the concussion shot is the set-up, for it requires that you first "tree" the gnome. Although treeing a gnome may seem like

a lot of work, your efforts will be rewarded in that you may, by way of a successful concussion shot, bag the gnome *live and uninjured*. Gnomes are excellent climbers. Given a chance to select between a morning spent in a hound's jaws or in the branches of a nearby oak tree, they pick the latter every time. But because gnomish bellies are fat and gnomish arms are short, their technique leaves them laid flat and still against the tree trunk, gripping the bark tightly with their thick little fingers. Take your opportunity here. Aim just to one side of the gnome's head, such that your shot hits the tree. Even a strong gnome will fall immediately and can be collected in a bag once it hits the ground. When the concussion shot is used against squirrels and other smaller arboreal creatures, it will kill them. The gnome's fortitude is great, however, and it is merely knocked unconscious by the bullet's reverberating impact in the tree and, subsequently, its skull. The fall shouldn't break any of your prey's sturdy bones. Death does a double take and leaves the gnome completely intact with no ill effects beyond an aching head, once it awakens.

Of course, the results of a botched concussion shot can be disastrous. If your aim has been tainted by a few early morning whiskies and you actually score a bullet to the gnome's skull, then no gnome. Hit too far to either side of the gnome's head, and your shot will miss the tree, possibly connecting with another member of your gnoming party. Depending on how your season is going, it's conceivably better to hit your partner, as any partaker of gnomish meat will attest.

Once bagged, gnomes must be stored if they are not to be served for that night's dinner. Expired gnomes can be hung in the cellar for up to a week or kept in the freezer for thawing later in the year. Keeping live gnomes is trickier. Hurry home with your catch before it comes to from the concussion shot. Many a hunter has shaken his head in dismay after his gnome woke up and slipped out of the bag using evil magic. Gnomes are also clever riddlers and are not above using such trickery to fool the unwitting sharpshooter into letting them go.

Don't be deceived. Get your gnome home and shackle it in the cellar before the creature opens its treacherous eyes. Small iron bands and chains will keep the gnome from using any of its magic, let alone digging its way out of its prison of stone. If you have been fortunate enough to catch a brace of gnomes, or if you are slowly amassing a collection, a damp barrel with a removable lid may be a more convenient storage method. Feed the gnomes radishes and beer, and they will remain docile, no matter how many of them you cram into the barrel.

Gnomes freshly dispatched — be they from field or barrel — must be drawn and skinned before they are fit for cooking. Their clothing, especially the hat, makes for a decent conversation starter, but for goodness' sake wash it all thoroughly before displaying. You have no idea where it's been. Unscrupulous hunters turn over gnome beards on the black market, but I find this practice loathsome, for even the most comprehensively boiled beard is still prone to harbouring pests. Handle yours with care, and dispose of it as you would vermin.

The meat of gnomes is lean, flavourful, and dense. As with all wild game, it is prone to dryness and is best prepared with an olive oil marinade, adding onions and thyme or rosemary before putting it in the oven. A quick roasting along the lines of that for a hare or pheasant of comparable size is the easiest way to cook your gnome, the simplicity of the process allowing its natural succulence to come to the fore. Long-bearded gnomes have a tendency to make for tough eating and are better suited to the stewpot than the roasting pan. Adding a handful of cubed bacon can bring back any moisture lost to age, and the pork develops in the gnome a flavour irresistible to nearly everyone squeamish about tasting wild game. The carcass and giblets are excellent bases for a soup stock.

As with much in the way of incorporating fairies into one's diet, the field of gnome cookery is an underdeveloped one. Experiment.

The Trouble of Trolls

No gnomer should go afield without keeping in mind that modern man is not the only enemy of the gnome. As the gnomish population has decreased, the danger posed to man by our prey's natural predator has risen. The trolls are hungry, and they are on the move. A single troll is more of a nuisance than twenty gnomes, but as a single troll is also stronger than twenty men and offers up not one scrap of tasty meat, "trolling" simply isn't much fun compared to gnoming. However, the problem remains, and the modern gnomer must come to grips with this reality.

Trolls are extremely sensitive to sunlight, a single ray of it turning them to stone, and so most of them retire hours before sunrise. Common sense tells us then that the easiest way to avoid crossing paths with a troll is to opt for gnoming at dawn rather than at dusk. Eventually, though, most gnomers will find themselves enjoying a spot of night gnoming, and in this a little knowledge of trolls can never hurt.

Fortunately, trolls are generally heard and smelt long before they are seen. The troll's utter lack of stalking skills and general absence of coordination make it impossible for this engine of destruction to sneak up on a hunter. The deafening crash of trees and the troll's thunderous bellowing and grunting signal its coming long before it arrives. Additionally, the odour of a mature troll is robust enough to pierce the thickest coat of elderberry paste. There's no need to go into specifics here—once the gnomer has caught a whiff of his first troll, he'll never mistake the smell for anything else.

Unfortunately, most people don't get a second chance to smell a troll. This is why the intelligent gnomer always has his elephant gun at the ready. The troll is a swift runner, but is slow to react when a cannon is pulled on him. As with gnomes, aim for the head. Strike anywhere else, and you'll be eating your own leg as a late-night snack.

Should you find yourself face-to-face with such a monster with nary an elephant gun at hand, as once happened to me, it is possible to dispatch the troll using the gnome's natural defence—the "difficult" riddle. Here's the one I employed to stunning effect against my troll: If one train departs Bradford at four o'clock and another departs Brighton at five o'clock, and the two trains arrive in Bristol at eight o'clock, then at what time did the trains arrive in Bristol? Something along these lines will cause the troll to stop whatever it is doing and sit to ponder the riddle until the strain of thought causes its head to explode. Stand clear, good sir.

AN IRON NAIL IN YOUR POCKET

The Joy of Rambling • The Nature of the Pixie • Glamour • The Home Tailor • The Iron Rod Campaign • Stray Sods • A Cautionary Tale

MANY PASTIMES HAVE BEEN described as quintessential to the country gentleman, among them rowing, golf, and occasional forays into plein-air watercolour. But none of these activities captures the full spectrum of the country gentleman's love for the landscape as does rambling.

When I speak of the rambler, I talk not of the boorish teller of tales sat by the fire at the village pub but rather of the devoted explorer and scholar of the byways which criss-cross the land. With sensible boots on feet and sturdy walking stick in hand, he can be found of an afternoon traversing field and footpath, connecting the dots on his Ordnance Survey map as he moves from gate to tumulus, from ancient tree to venerable cenotaph, taking in fresh countryside air and the rays of the sun whilst navigating the earth completely on his own terms.

But is his tread truly his own? Are there aspects of this simplest of activities, of putting one foot in front of the other, over which the rambler has not utter command? I'm unhappy to report that indeed there are. Of course, some of these features are generally innocuous and are what make a walk interesting, the day's weather being the most pervasive and variable, with topography and the region's flora and fauna also making the list. The animals in most parts of the civilised world are, generally speaking, docile and unthreatening, as eager to keep their distance from your garden-variety rambler as they are from the game warden and the sportsman. Anyone enjoying vigorous time outside looks upon all these factors not as impediments to an afternoon well spent but as intriguing features to be cherished for giving the day's stroll its characteristic flavour.

But for all his innocent joy, the countryside rambler attracts a new element — or shall I say a new *elemental* — keen on spoiling the pastime. Let this essay serve as an education to the rambler who would be prepared for a meeting with the most prevalent fairy to be found choking the countryside path — the pixie.

Found historically in Cornwall, the pixie is distributed throughout a territory thought by this author to be expanding to encompass all of southwestern Britain, as evidenced by the disoriented souls I have encountered on otherwise unhorrifying walks in Devon and Dorset. Pixies are ethereal in nature, though, and this has hindered efforts at maintaining an accurate accounting of their population and range.

In their regular form, which is composed of pure light and energy, pixies are nearly invisible to our eyes and, for the most part, harmless. In this state they appear only as flashes of brightness that may as well be glints of sunlight gleaming off the rim of a newly polished bucket, so fleeting and swift are their movements. It is when the pixie coagulates itself, through an intense concentration tainted with what one might call malice, that it is able to interact with its environment to the point that it becomes a bother.

That these otherwise giddy creatures are most likely to be found inhabiting morbid locales such as the battlegrounds and burial sites of the early tribes should come as no surprise to the thoughtful rambler, who may simply add this fact to his already overstuffed file of evidence proving the perverse nature of Fairyland's most dedicated meddlers.

The pixies seem to have no aim in life save the endless playing of pranks. 'Twas ever thus. The first written account of such trouble is from a source no less venerable than Tacitus, describing the bedevilings of the pixies upon the Roman legions. For any of my readers who consider themselves more prepared than an armoured phalanx of disciplined legionnaires to meet the tricky ways of the tribal fey, perhaps this essay is superfluous. For the rest of you, read on.

Today, the puckish predilections of the pixies are apparent in the continual mischief they visit upon the progress of innocent country ramblers. Through speed, a surprising strength (given the fact that the largest of pixies stands no taller than the top of a

Chelsea boot), and their ability to enchant humans into thinking no mischief is afoot, pixies are able to pull stunts such as switching a rambler's shoes, turning a held walking stick upside down, or even replacing one Ordnance Survey map with another *whilst it is being read*. Any of these attempts at pixie "humour" results in irritation in the best of circumstances, that is, if it is even noticed. At their worst, pixie pranks can disguise pits, bogs, and cliff-sides such that they appear to be pleasant paths or meadows, a situation which could lead to serious injury or worse should the rambler set foot into these misleading landscapes.

One of the pixie's favourite tricks is to employ *glamour* against the senses of its human victims. Glamour is the power of illusion, a magic which makes things appear differently—more beautiful and enticing, in most instances—than they truly are. Such sorcery is common at fairy revels, transforming otherwise lacklustre hillsides into miniature palaces complete with ballrooms and banquet halls brimming with delights. Should the proceedings happen to be interrupted by mortals, the entire sumptuous scene can vanish in the blink of an eye. Glamour is most dangerous in that what it portrays is in fact real, but only so long as its victim believes it to be so. Food made of glamour, for instance, can be eaten and will taste delicious, even going so far as to provide sustenance to its eater, *until* he becomes aware that it was but illusion. At that point the food and any nourishment obtained by it transmute instantly to cold ash. This turnabout can be especially unfortunate if the eater has been living off glamour for more than a few days.

Many a rambler has paused after stooping to tie an errant bootlace or after swatting away a strange insect, disturbed by a subtle change in their surroundings that they can't quite put their finger on. It is easy to dismiss this initial feeling of something being amiss, to fall prey to the pixie's trickery. But one must remain alert and shake off the spell in its first stages. Here are some tested suggestions for the rambler who would be ready for the pranks of the pixie.

The traditional practice of turning one's jacket inside out to deflect pixie enchantments is effective, but is one I've always found distasteful, as it spoils the utility of the coat and the general appearance of the rambler. Personally, I've taken to plucking out the thread from the interior labels of my walking jackets, then with deft needle reapplying them to the corresponding location on the exterior. Apart from this aberration, my coats appear fine to all observers save the pixies, who see that my clothes must already be inside out. To them, I have obviously already been tricked—"pixilated," some say—and so they offer me no trouble. All the same, this is not an option for the unskilled home tailor, and I believe a general letter-writing initiative ought to be undertaken to the manufacturers of the best rambling outerwear, bringing the issue of pixies to their attention and proposing that anti-fey alterations be introduced—at least as an option—henceforth.

However, sitting at home pricking one's ink-stained fingertips with sewing needles is not the optimal way for the rambling enthusiast to spend his idle hours. Should the pixies see us reduced to such a state, they would but redouble their efforts at pranksterism, and soon there would be no hope for reclaiming the footpaths from them. No, this is a situation which calls not for meekness but for a show of countering force, one using equally effective and proven means against the pixies.

The Iron Rod Campaign

In the long timeline of the Fairy Kingdom, iron is a relatively recent invention. Like other innovations of the rationally superior man, it has proven time and time again to be the bane of the fey. For this reason, fairies such as pixies tend to avoid iron gates and even footpath stiles constructed using iron nails, and so these places can provide ample sanctuary for the rambler plagued by pixies.

Iron nails embody all the qualities of the metal in a supremely handy and utilitarian form. Employed to best advantage whilst enjoying a tramp through fen and forest, an iron nail is a boon companion. Simply carrying such a nail in the pocket of your hiking trousers reduces the likelihood of encountering any solitary pixies haunting the path.

But if you'd like a stronger insurance policy against the pixie's malice, or if you fear your walk will take you through territory positively riddled with them, more resolute measures are called for.

One particularly effective way to incorporate anti-fey tactics into your ramble is to carry a walking stick fitted with an iron ferrule sharpened to a keen spike. As it punctures the soil at every other step on your walk, this tool drives literal holes into the plots of the pixie pranksters. Such a walking stick helps even as it swings alongside the rambler. With each pass through the air, the iron tip traces a line of turbulent energy unbreachable by pixies. The line is faint, to be sure, and fades over time, but imagine the cumulative disruptive effect should all countryside enthusiasts use iron-tipped walking canes. Happy is the rambler who does so much good for his fellow man simply by walking about. For those activists among us (and I am one), why not acquire a walking stick made entirely of the stuff? Its heft may reduce the number of miles you feel like walking on a particular day, to be sure,

goblinproofing one's chicken coop

but its presence virtually guarantees protection against being waylaid by pixies. If you find yourself veering in the direction of the hand holding the walking stick, just switch from left to right every so often, or best of all, carry a metre-length of iron in each hand, as I am wont to do when popping round sites of historical interest known to be infested by pixies. It takes a while to get the movement figured out—it's a bit like cross-country skiing, actually—but imagine my peace of mind as I contribute to the disruption of pixie trickery *and* get a ferocious upper-body workout to boot.

A cousin of the pixie, the detestable creature known as the *stray sod* employs a more direct approach to mucking things up, as it were, on the trail. Disguised as a divot of grass-topped turf indistinguishable from those commonly found along rural footpaths, the stray sod is practised at a specific sort of enchantment. When trod upon, accidentally or otherwise, this fairy poisons the rambler's mind with a sudden sense of misdirection. This confusion is known as being "pixie-led." Landmarks disappear from view under this influence, and well-known fields lose their familiarity. For ramblers not averse to wearing crampons, the iron spikes will deter the most pestiferous of stray sods, as the tufted troublemakers are as fatally allergic to iron as are the common pixies.

If, after reading all of the above, you remain unconvinced of the urgent need to rise up against the pixies and their puckish ways, a final anecdote may fill you with the required resolve.

The contributions of early twentieth-century naturalist and watercolourist Angus McAnnis are known to every schoolboy. What is frightfully under-reported is the manner of his demise. McAnnis was out for a tramp in southern Cornwall, accompanied by members of a local artists' society hoping to glean a bit of his talent and wisdom. At an opportune moment, pixies infiltrated the walking party, silently snatching the map McAnnis was holding and replacing it with one made entirely of glamour. The map led McAnnis and his walking companions flawlessly for several miles but then suggested a route so erratic and outlandish that the party was given over to impassioned disagreement as to its accuracy. A headstrong fellow, McAnnis was not to be swayed by his compatriots' pleas to turn back and around dusk struck out on his own, head buried in the deceitful folds of his map of glamour, feet in thrall to the landmarks it appeared to indicate. The rest of the walking party realised the truth too late when, having doubled back, they found McAnnis's original map, soiled and half eaten by mouths no larger than those of shrews, near where the confusion had begun. His body was never recovered, but the remains of the map now reside in the permanent collection of the Ramblers' main office in London.

It is hoped that the above tale provides all readers who love the countryside enough in the way of grim encouragement in our mutual fight against the meddlesome, sometimes deadly, forces of the fey.

FAERIE-FORAGING

*Foraging Today • The Solitary Fairies •
Truffle-Hunting in Ireland • Hopes Dashed •
A Friend in Peril • Momentary Gains • A Repulsive
Revival • Home and Back Again •
All That Glitters*

UNTIL RECENTLY, THE INCLUSION of a chapter on foraging in a guidebook such as this would have been quite a different affair, one of encouraging people to discover the delectable treasures of the hedgerow and forest after what had been a few generations of neglect. But happily, more and more countryside ramblers are incorporating a bit of food-gathering into their outings, and so instructional essays can now go into further detail about the delights—and dangers—awaiting resourceful foragers.

Chief among the threats the modern forager faces is that of interference from representatives of the "solitary fairies." Somerset's indigenous Apple Tree Man and the Ghillie Dhu of Scotland are but two examples of these fey, whose lives are fixated upon the jealous guarding of the fruits of their respective regions. As the forests and other wild habitations of the solitary fairies have diminished and thinned over the centuries, this incredibly long-lived population has found itself in closer and closer quarters, such that the solitary fey are not only encountered more often on one's berry-picking outings, but they are also more keen on hoarding for themselves what fruits, nuts, and edible mushrooms are to be found. The forest's bounty belongs as much to man as it does to the birds and beasts and certainly as much as it does to the stingy fey, who take so much and give so little in return.

There are shelves and shelves of manuals detailing what wild food grows in your local region and the best times of the year to find it. Ubiquitous too are guidebooks on which fairies lurk in which parts of the countryside, what bits of the plant kingdom they protect, and how best to supplicate to these gangsterish Green Men. You know where to find such information, and so it is not my work to reprint it here.

What the modern hedgerow-hunter wants is an update on the legends, a first-hand report of the

dangers of the solitary fey and how disaster at their hands is no more than one or two paces away for the incautious forager. I'm somewhat reluctant to tell the following story, as things didn't work out exactly as I'd planned. But I do believe it illustrates a modicum of what we're all up against when we forage in fairy country.

If one were — preposterously, I'll admit — a representative of the Irish sparrowhawk population out for an autumn afternoon's soar high above the fields outside Belfast a few years ago, one could have spotted two chestnut-coloured patches of tweed picking their way among the thickening forest. These specks were in fact a pair of men in search of the elusive corvus truffle, a jet-black variety which had reappeared after a 150-year absence. I'd tasted my first one a week earlier at a posh restaurant in town and thought the flavour so indescribably scrumptious that I had to have some for myself. To that end I'd engaged as co-conspirator a good friend of mine, a chef and rival restaurateur of international renown, whom for reasons of discretion I must refer to simply as "Tom." Our first order of business had been to liquor up said restaurant's recently sacked sous-chef, who in his drunkenness had let slip the coordinates where we might likely find the mother lode of this particular fungus.

And so there we were, wellies on feet and mycology guidebooks in hand, combing over the bosky, jade-tinted landscape in search of the rare and priceless corvus. I was brimming with optimism, and so had brought along a large canvas sack which I hoped would soon be topped up with succulent truffles.

We were also enjoying draws from a particularly potent flask of Tom's own cherry brandy, which I was sinking into perhaps a bit more quickly than usual on account of my companion's ceaseless jabbering. He had no equal in the kitchen, this man, but he was no deerstalker. Nor much of a truffler, I was discovering, as we'd been out several hours and hadn't turned up a single specimen of the fungus under any of the oak trees where it was purported to grow. We'd spotted our next contender growing at the base of a wooded hillside, however, and were making our way towards the tree. I'd straggled a bit, or at least feigned straggling, letting Tom crash on through the brambles several paces ahead. He seemed happy enough to lumber on without me, as

oblivious to the underbrush as he was to any semblance of proper flow in our conversation.

The oak was possessed of an impressive girth,
suggesting it must have been one of the older giants
of the forest. Tom flattened the bracken beneath him
as he rounded it, his eyes sweeping the forest floor
for signs of our quarry nestling in the underbrush.
He was going on about the scientific underpinnings
of symbiosis and "the marvel of inorganic nitrogen
absorption" or some such rot when he stopped,
mid-stride and mid-sentence, his gaze rooted to the
ground just the other side of the tree. I was sure he'd

found our sought-for treasure trove, as a moment later he fairly exploded with "Blimey! Is that what I think it is?"

But what silver-rimmed hope for truffles gleamed in my mind's eye tarnished the moment I heard, from the back of the massive oak, a most unsettling reply to dear Tom's question. For it was then that the crystalline quiet of the Irish forest shattered into a thousand shards as a peal of chittering—much like a red squirrel's, actually—met my ear, followed by a rapid cadence of tinny tinks.

If you've had the opportunity to really delve into the story of the tragic fate of the RMS *Titanic*, itself a tale of Irish woe and calamity, then you might have a sense of the icy dread which struck my heart at that moment, breaching the hull of my dreams of a leisurely afternoon spent mushroom hunting. Now the engine room of my soul began to fill with a terror most dire. My left hand closed tightly on my guidebook and my right hand shot reflexively towards my hip, where it was dismayed to discover that I'd cavalierly left my hunting pistol at home. It was an omission which had made perfect sense during the day's preparations—this afternoon was meant to be spent bagging truffles, after all, not stumpy green-clad cobblers.

My mouth recalled the flavour of the last leg-of-leprechaun I'd enjoyed, nearly washing away the tang of dread I now experienced standing just out of sight of the most vicious of Ireland's solitary fairies.

Don't get me wrong. I wouldn't have been surprised to find that Tom knew his way around a leprechaun quite handily in the kitchen, but I assumed that the only one he'd ever contended with would have been delivered to him atop a bed of ice, not sat gaily upon its own forest workbench, hammer at the ready. And although biting into a properly prepared roast leprechaun is inarguably the pinnacle experience one may have whilst enjoying Hibernian cuisine, having it the other way round — with leprechaun biting into you — is in no way comparable. It's just nowhere near as pleasant. They've got phenomenal dental integrity, and their bites are remarkable at harbouring infection in the parts of their victims which remain intact.

All it took was the sight of Tom bending down and extending his arm with a cheerful "'ello, little fellow!" to tell me he had no idea of the depth of his peril. And so I felt absolutely no regret at that moment racing round the tree and whizzing a medium-sized stone straight past Tom's head and squarely into the countenance of the leering leprechaun. It was out cold in an instant, its tapered kelly green hat still stuck atop its head in a most eerie fashion.

With the attentions of the ruddy-cheeked marauder now transported to wherever it is they roam when unconscious, I turned to my foraging partner and, drawing in a deep breath and straightening my posture, prepared to level a scathing education at the man, one outlining the precise dangers of any attempts to shake hands with a chittering leprechaun. But the stunned look on Tom's face as he stood up told me he already knew. He shook his head quickly, no doubt to disperse the effects of the leprechaun's ability to charm those unused to its malicious tendencies.

"Is it dead?" my innocent companion asked.

"Not in the slightest," I replied. "Fantastically difficult creatures to kill, leprechauns. Can withstand all manner of injury and keep going. The stone in the face was just a lucky moment for me, and for you! Had that toothy tinkerer got hold of your arm with its jaws, we might well have had to amputate. Thankfully, they're always found alone, one of the 'solitary fairies,' taxonomically speaking, chiefly on account of their breath. Once the carcass is cleaned, though, leprechauns make famous eating, no trace of harmful bacteria or poison in the meat itself. I haven't got any sporting way of killing it, though. Didn't bring a firearm on this forage. But they often guard treasure of one sort or another, so we're going to have to move quickly and ascertain its holdings before it comes to."

Indeed, what came into focus now that we were free to exist without immediate threat from the red-bearded ruffian was a lush patch of the very truffle we'd been searching for, the ebony corvus truffles spread in great profusion among the season's first fallen leaves. I got to work immediately, as did Tom, and we filled to bursting the sack we'd brought with spongy wonders, dreaming of the meals Tom could prepare with them back at the restaurant. When the bag could hold no more, I tied it tight with a hand-kerchief and grabbed a few more of the mushrooms, stuffing them into my jacket pockets.

Although I muttered that he might not want to do so, Tom picked up the leprechaun's tiny hammer and the filthy boot it had been working on, turning them over in his hands.

"They're not much for cobblers," I said. "Of course, hardly anyone has shoes worth mending anymore, but if you look closely, you'll see some characteristic elements of fey craftsmanship which, if not beautiful, are ingeniously practical. If they weren't so bloody delicious, it would be easier to see leprechauns as nearly manlike. Like some birds and primates, they use tools. But leprechauns take things a bit further, repurposing found objects into their work. I'll bet we can find some such effort put into this boot." I stepped over to Tom and folded the boot open. "Do you see how it's used an old bottle cap here to make the grommet? It's that sort of inventiveness which makes leprechauns fascinating."

It was sloppy of me, getting distracted by the handiwork, almost as though the boot itself carried some taint of the leprechaun's charm. The quick crunching of leaves we heard at that moment might as well have been the sound of our dreams for a peaceful departure from the forest being wadded up and thrown into the rubbish bin. I spun round towards the direction of the noise and fell backwards as an emerald blur shot past me and collided at chest level with the ill-prepared Tom who, dropping the boot and falling to the ground, commenced a vigorous struggling under the manic attentions of the leprechaun.

I snatched up the sackful of truffles. A voice in my head told me to run, but to do so would have left Tom to an indescribable fate. Many years in the kitchen had made him a stout man, and fit, but I could tell he was no match for the leprechaun with its wiry strength and hell-bent bloodlust.

I had found myself upon a truly sticky wicket and was confronted with a choice: On the one hand, here I was set up for a good long while with a sack of mushrooms any gourmand would give his left arm for. On the other hand, there was poor Tom, flat on the ground and *actually* about to give up his left arm, without a single truffle to show for it.

I wished to give careful deliberation to my next move. This decision required thought. Hands fumbled kerchief, and I loosed the mouth of the sack, yanking it open and peering down into its betruffled depths. As I moved the bag around, the corvus truffles rolled lazily over one another, performing languid motions worthy of a Moroccan belly dancer, so full and ripe they were, so eager to imbue my life with pleasure. The truffles' musky odour rose from the sack and filled the Bakeley nostrils. Theirs was an earthy scent which, once the mushrooms had been sliced and sautéed in butter, would grow and bloom into delight unmatched by any other. All this rapture was quite literally within my grasp, and as I imagined the promised dinner, I heard the truffles call my name. "Reginald . . . Reginald . . ."

My reverie was short-lived, however, broken by a sharp kick against my shin. "Reginald!" shrieked the still-beleaguered Tom, prostrate at my feet, the fierce leprechaun gamely struggling at his arm, face, or wherever else it might be granted a toothy purchase. Looking over the edge of the sack at my friend's anguished face robbed me of the joy I'd been soaking in a moment earlier. "Reginald! You've got to help me! Please!"

And as the clouds fogging my mind's eye parted, I realised Tom was right. Action must be taken at once if there was any hope for happiness to reign that day. With one last glance at the mushrooms, I upturned the bag, returning its contents to the earth, and in a single swift motion brought down the empty sack on the leprechaun, catching it up and closing the top, secured once more by the handkerchief. It hurt like the dickens for things to turn out this way, but the thought of losing Tom was what changed my mind. That man knows his way around a saucepan, and with him gone I would be high and dry, with no one to bring these impossibly mouth-watering mushrooms to their full potential.

I reached down and helped him to his feet.

"All right then?" I asked the rumpled gourmet as he brushed soil and leaves from his face, hair, coat, and trousers, wheezing heavily as he did. "You don't seem to have suffered any leprechaun bites. If you're feeling fit, then help me gather up as much of this scattered treasure as we can carry in our arms. We won't be able to haul off as many truffles as the sack held, I'm afraid, but . . ."

Tom stood before me, still panting some and, despite his brushings, looking yet for all the world like John the Baptist, right down to that wild look in

goblinproofing one's chicken coop

his eyes. I could tell he wasn't listening. Tom simply never did pick up a knack for conversation.

I went on regardless.

"We could bring home half a peck if we think resourcefully." I reached for my collar in order to shrug off my coat and use it as a makeshift sack, but Tom's hand on my shoulder stopped me. His was a trembling hand, yet strong.

"Reg." There was a dead seriousness about his gaze. "I nearly died. That thing wasn't going to back down. It was going to kill me." His stare was that of a desperate man, one who needs reassuring.

"Yes, but we showed it who's on top, didn't we?" I gave the writhing sack a playful kick. "Our chittering little friend is snug and secure in that bag. He won't be able to get out until we want him to. He's a lively one, though. In fact, I believe we should carry him back to town and hang him up in the kitchen for later, then get three more sacks and return here and fill them with truffles."

"I forbid you to bring any of those evil mushrooms into my kitchen, Reginald Bakeley!" Tom was clearly still in the thrall of the adrenaline brought on by his little scuffle. "I don't want that leprechaun anywhere near me. I don't want another thing to do with that monster, nor its truffles!"

I sensed that what this moment wanted was a bit of strategy. "Everything is fine, my friend," I replied. "Let's leave all this here, retrace our steps, and get you home again." Tom seemed to relax a bit at this, and as I walked him back up the hillside, I was careful to take several purposeful looks around.

Within an hour I'd taken Tom home, secured him in his easy chair with blanket and tea cup, promised to check on him the next morning, and returned to the oak tree, pistol in hand and a half-dozen flour sacks I'd conscripted from Tom's kitchen thrown over my shoulder. The oak was still standing where I'd left it, but nothing else about the scene remained the same. There was no trace of the captured leprechaun, nor signs of our tussle, nor even a single truffle in sight anywhere. I checked all round the tree and rummaged through piles of leaves, to no avail.

Thoroughly confused and not a little upset at being robbed of both the truffles and the possibility of a roast leg-of-leprechaun (for in my experience, revenge is a dish best served piping hot, with a garnish), back to town I went. At the very least I could surprise Tom with the fistfuls of mushrooms I'd stashed away in our initial raid, show him that our nerve-wracking afternoon hadn't been without reward. But once hands entered pockets, they closed round small, hard masses of a most unexpected texture. Had the truffles dried out so quickly? I pulled the lumps out and looked at them. They were no longer mushrooms, to be sure, but seemed to be nuggets of purest gold.

"Blast that cobbler!" I shouted, hoping that if the leprechaun could hear me he would at least give a sniggering laugh to indicate the direction in which I ought to point my pistol. But no such sound came in reply. The gold felt hard and cold in my hands, a derisive pay-off meant to keep me from biting into one of those tender, mysterious mushrooms.

I briefly considered returning to the restaurant in Belfast and offering to buy their entire stockpile of the magical truffles, then thought better of it. To do so would only be admitting defeat. Maybe I could use the gold to bribe Tom into coming with me on another forage. But even a sackful of nuggets like those I held in my quivering hands wouldn't be enough to bring me the pleasure of cooking up my own pan of the leprechaun's truffles, if not the leprechaun itself.

I turned in the direction of home, the gears and springs of my mind already churning away at a plot whereby I might one day get another crack at the treasure which had so cunningly eluded me.

THE UNCANNY
COMPANION

*The Faerie-Double • Face-Off • The Tolling of the
Bell • Recollections of the Morning • The Road
Home • Waylaid • The Sluagh • Staring into the
Abyss • Remedy and Revival*

I REMEMBER THE MOMENT with crystal clarity. There, not four feet from the end of my nose, stood a fiendish apparition. It shuddered in and out of sight, listing some, as though struggling to remain upright on the deck of some storm-tossed ghost ship on a distant sea, a befogged vessel whose sails and mast were visible to him alone. Yet despite the ghastly haze which separated us, I was still able to catch squarely the look of disdain on the spirit's face. It was as though this ghost was mocking me for a lifetime of thought and action that he would have — had he been free to walk the sunlit world as I have, not being relegated as he was to Faerie's shadowy underworld — conducted somewhat differently.

This half-tangible wraith meant to frighten me, but I wasn't about to take the bait. I mean, really, who among us has found themselves on a week-long holiday in the Scottish Highlands and *not* had to contend from time to time with such a spirit? To be startled the first time or two, rattled even, is natural. But the trick I've learned when facing off against the contemptuous apparition that is one's *fetch*, or faerie-double, is this: Show no weakness. Establish dominance from the outset, and maintain it.

And so I brought myself to my full height, straightened my waistcoat, and shot the deceptively handsome stranger a grin that was at once knowing and withering. It was a technique I'd perfected at Eton, and I'd found opportunity to practise it now and again as an adult. The fetch stared back at me, its face twisted into a similar, ineffective sneer.

"You think you've got me all sorted out, don't you?" I spat. "Well, let me tell you, I know a thing or two about *fetches*." The fetch said nothing, although its mouth did move to ape my own speaking, and as I turned and began to pace, my own gaze not once breaking from that of the sinister spirit's, I saw, through the murky, mystic scrim separating our worlds, my double do the same. No matter, that. The fetch is an expert at mind games, but I was feeling confident.

"I suppose you think I ought to be frightened," I continued, "that perhaps I should go run and hide and cravenly tremble over the doom which you portend? What is it, foul *doppelgänger*, that you wish me to believe? That I'm about to lose a loved one? That I myself am in mortal danger this evening?" The fetch gesticulated in grave duplication of my own calculated flailings. "Let me tell you something which you apparently fail to understand, grim phantom. I am a man who has seen things, things which would terrify the strongest of men had they not, as I have, grown so dreadfully used to them! I've perforated giants four times your size with poisoned darts, distracting the monsters with riddles and card tricks until the venom took effect. I've sidestepped the deadly affections of the *glaistig*, that foul succubus of a fairy woman. Broke her heart in two, in fact. I've even eaten a plate of medium-rare *nuckelavee*—one I stalked myself— *and enjoyed the taste!* The Second Sight may not be what I would have chosen as the defining feature of my life, but possess it I do and cower from it and all the miserable horrors it brings before my eyes I do not! So just because you think you can frighten me with your leerings, your impish parody of my walk, and your foreshadowing by your very manifestation of some bad end which is to befall me, it doesn't mean that you can! I swear, fetch, I can hardly turn around without bumping into wights, ghouls, trolls, and bogeys, and now here *you* are, the most ridiculous of them all. You tire me, fetch.

You bore me senseless. So go, unquiet wanderer! Fly! Disperse yourself into the clammy night air from which you've congealed! You'll get no satisfaction from your intended victim tonight!"

I thought it would work, too, my being firm with the fetch. It was a tack which had served me well in many confrontations before. Yet there—coming into clearer focus, it seemed—still stood the double, a disgustingly smug look draped across its deceitful face and an attitude of absolute haughtiness shot through its frame (a smartly dressed one, too, I had to admit). This was the most defiant, the most self-assured, the most pompous specimen of bogey I had ever confronted. I'd just hit it square across the old

physiognomy with my best verbal lunge, and it had taken the blow without so much as a flinch. That the fetch wasn't coming back at me with a bone-shaking assault of its own was even more disconcerting. What *was* it thinking, and what indeed did it want with me tonight?

These thoughts and a dozen others scampered beneath the floorboards of my mind as I stepped towards the fetch, pinching my countenance into an impressive squint which I hoped would convey that I had discerned its true motive. As it had done for the entirety of our face-off, the double merely mimicked me, leaning forwards and glowering right back, until our equally well-proportioned noses were inches apart and I could feel its hot breath upon my face.

But from this close vantage point something became clearer. There was a weariness in the double's eyes, a fatigue I'd begun to feel a degree of myself. Was this another of the fetch's tricks, or was I actually beginning to wear down this dastardly spirit's defences? I drew in a deep breath, mentally piecing together my next forensic jab.

"Last call!" Derek the barman's shout burst through the door of the gentleman's water closet

where I stood. Instinctively I spun towards the summons, forgetting for an instant the terror which now stood behind me. And when I turned again, all I found was my own reflection staring back at me from the mirror above the sink.

Although I had been intensely curious to see what the fetch would do next, I must admit I felt some relief that the encounter had passed. With a swift adjustment of my crimson cravat and a pass of the fingers through the old Bakeley hair, I burst through the door in time to secure one last tipple from the good Derek. If a man can't feel safe and untroubled by his demons in the village public house, that bastion of civilisation and humanity, then where, I ask you, can he?

The only double I wanted to contend with at that moment was amber in colour and served neat. It was the work of but a moment to procure the final whisky, and that of two more to bring it to lip and tilt back the tumbler. The golden fluid, more intrinsic to the national character of Scotland than wine is to France, or aquavit to the Scandinavian countries, set about its work of restoring my composure in the wake of my contretemps with the fetch. I wondered how it was I felt so thoroughly flustered by the meeting. After all, I'd been drinking for hours.

I bade Derek a good night and, amidst the din of the night's closing bell, pushed myself out the front door of The Lamprey's Arms and into the blackness of the Caledonian night. I must say, with the exception of its being haunted, the Lamprey had been as enjoyable a place to spend a long evening as I'd hoped it would be. It came enthusiastically recommended to me by my host, the estimable Professor Marcus White, a man of science and a long-time associate who had called me up to his manor home on the shores of Loch Ness. The professor wanted to share with me some recent findings regarding the mineral properties of turf samples taken from fairy mounds near Aberfoyle. We'd had a jolly enough week of it, I suppose, squinting at the soil, and in a few days I was scheduled to return home. That morning, Marcus had mentioned a call he'd received to attend an impromptu conference between a group of fellow fairy researchers and, after assuring me that the meeting would be "utterly dreary, not at all interesting to a man of action such as yourself," hoped that I wouldn't mind having a full day on my own. I conceded that he was probably right and, having told him I was game for a long walk, took Marcus's suggestion that I visit the village of Felstane, situated about seven miles distant and known for its curious shops and convivial pub.

We ate breakfast, and the professor walked with me to the front hall, where I pulled on my smartest rambling boots. On the table near the door stood a large crystal vase I'd been admiring since I'd arrived. Not the vase itself, actually, so much as its contents — hundreds of the professor's cat's-eye marbles, each of them the size of a horse chestnut. As I slipped my arms into my walking jacket's sleeves, I ventured a glance at the collection.

"You like those, Reg. Why not pick one out for yourself?" said Marcus. I felt the colour rush to my cheeks; he'd caught me like a schoolboy, and I raised a clumsy objection.

"Go on, pick one out," he cajoled. "I like to keep one in my pocket at all times, don't you know. I find it focuses the mind, cuts out distraction." And with  that he reached his hand into the front pocket of his waistcoat and drew out a beauty of a shooter, the blue glass within it looking like the smoke from out the end of the evening's welcome pipe. It was no use struggling, I had to have one for myself. With one last look to Marcus as if to ask whether it really was all right, I lowered my hand into the vase and selected a marble, one with a curl of yellow reaching across its glassy diameter.

"Thank you, Marcus," I blurted. "It's a very fine collection."

"It's nothing, old friend," he replied. "I love them all, but I've got too many. I'm glad to see one go to a person I know can put it to thorough use." With a smile I dropped the sphere into my jacket's outer pocket. Between the marble and the flask of a favoured Highlands whisky I'd equipped in my jacket's inner breast pocket, I was completely prepared for the trek.

Thus composed I set out, following a network of footpaths connecting Professor White's loch-side home and the village. The exercise was invigorating, and I was glad for the chance to get in touch with the region's fabled landscape. I passed the morning as carefree as the finches darting through the skies above, trying my best to whistle their song. Near the midway point I took a short rest, striking up a conversation with a pair of workmen patching a stone wall, and from our talk I picked up a few notes of interest regarding variations in stone-building across the breadth of Scotland.

Once I reached the borders of Felstane, I popped into an antiques dealer's on the main road. I was in the midst of admiring a tidy platoon of lead soldiers which would complement my regiments back home when I was greeted by the proprietress, a woman possessed of advanced age and delightful facial asymmetry. She asked whether I was visiting from outside the village, and once I'd told her I was the guest of Professor White's, her eyes bulged in a most alarming manner.

"Ah, the professor! Wait right there, love. I've got some things you and the professor will find *fascinating.*" She disappeared into the next room, and when she returned carrying a good-sized wooden chest, I stepped towards her and offered to help her with it. "Sit down, sit down. I've got it," she replied, setting the box on a table. I took a seat.

The moment she began to open the chest I remembered a warning Marcus had given me earlier in the week, but it was too late for me to flee now. Apparently, his work has made him somewhat of a celebrity among the local villagers, who do a brisk business in the trafficking of counterfeit Faerie artifacts. And now, having let slip his name, it seemed I was fated to spend a good portion of my day in Felstane turning down one after another of these ersatz atrocities. It was pitiable, really, seeing this otherwise respectable merchant haul out a tiny pair of crutches and tell me they once belonged to a Cornish spriggan, or to watch her unfold an admittedly well-made shawl and claim it was woven with strands of elfin hair. I was able to extricate myself from this ghoulish parade only after repeated insistence that I wasn't in the market for a reddish wool cap purportedly stolen from the border goblins. I neglected to tell her I already had seven of them hanging in my trophy case at home.

Whereas the banter with the workmen had been charming and edifying, the conversation with the antiques dealer had soured the day, and I went straight to the Lamprey's Arms, taking a late lunch and easing into the evening's tipple a bit early.

As I walked the midnight road home, these meetings and that with my eerie fairy-double all muddled and blended together in my mind somewhat, facilitated no doubt by the final drink at the pub. I slipped my hand into my jacket pocket and closed it round the marble. The professor was right; the mere act of grasping the cool glass brought a good deal of clarity to my thoughts. My consciousness surfaced from the depths of my meditations, and I noticed just ahead on the path the stone wall I'd passed that morning. Even in the dark I could see that the job hadn't been completed. It didn't seem the workmen had done anything more to it since our talk, actually. This was curious, as they'd been labouring rather intently when I'd paused to speak with them. I shook my head and trudged on, happy in the thought I was halfway to the professor's house.

The whisky generously continued to lend a good deal of its warming effect to my bones, and I stoked its fire with a few long swigs from my flask. I'd been on countless walks such as this one, and whilst my thoughts typically fixate on what's going into the garden next or on the upcoming sporting season, tonight—perhaps as a result of my close shave back in the Lamprey's water closet—I couldn't help but think of the legends of late-night fairy encounters along the roads of this bogey-peppered neck of the woods. From out of the twin murks of the dim path before me and my whisky-dampened mind emerged the story of the *fachan*, a pogo-stick sort of fellow with naught but one leg, one arm, and a single eye, who hops about frightening the odd nocturnal rambler. I also reflected on the nature of the *urisk*, a dour character with no particular itinerary of an evening, other than the leading of travellers off the footpath and down the face of some rocky cliffside. Bloody inconsiderate things, urisks, bothering innocent people who are only trying to get home.

I realised my mind was wandering again. It was the whisky, I suppose, knocking about in the Bakeley bloodstream. My hand slid towards my jacket pocket for another grab at the marble, but when it got there, my fingers grasped nothing but thin air.

This alone would have been cause for alarm, had I not at that very moment been distracted by a sharp growl and the scuttling sounds of some creature just off the side of the path to my right. The noise diminished, moving away from me in the direction I'd just come. My attention fully focused, I extracted from the recesses of my memory a stack of mental index cards I keep there listing the small- to medium-sized fauna of this particular region of Scotland. This I flipped through in my mind, trying in vain to determine what could have rushed off through the underbrush in such a manner. Badger, *baobhan sith*, barnacle goose, *bean nighe*, black grouse, *bodach* . . . none presented itself as an exact match for a creature which might have made the sounds I'd heard.

The breeze picked up, and I felt as though an icicle had been dropped down the back of my collar. I retied the cravat about my neck and pulled my jacket tight, doubling my pace. If I was about to be caught in one of the Highlands' sudden storms, I'd rather be that much closer to my destination. At least there was some comfort in walking with my back to the growing wind, which now carried on it a high-pitched whine that quickly grew to a piercing wail.

Something tiny and muscular began struggling beneath my cravat, in the vicinity of my jugular vein. I tore at the scarf, keen on getting at whatever insect had lodged itself there. But before I could do so, I found myself flailing the cloth about my head, swatting away at a black cloud of clegs, the monstrous horseflies of the Highlands. Where had they come from? With my other hand fast across my nose and mouth to keep any from getting in, I batted desperately against the swarm. On the occasions I ventured a breath, my mouth filled with greasy, foul-tasting gulps of air.

Through the insect fog a new sound became apparent, a mixed cacophony of hollers and shrieks. These grew louder and, as the din broke into distinct, untranslatable cries and screeches, a blunt force against my hip knocked me to the ground. Reduced to all fours and gagging on a pair of unfortunate clegs, I looked up the path in disbelief at what appeared to be the elderly antiques dealer from the village, utterly naked and with a long, ragged cloud of dust-coloured hair streaking behind her. She sat astride an old shovel, blade foremost, which itself hovered about four feet above the earth.

The cloud of flies dispersed, and as I stood back up, I was able to spit one of the horseflies from my mouth. I could only assume I'd swallowed the other. The witch performed a few jagged aerial manoeuvres and then, regaining her balance and pointing the shovel's blade in my direction, gave her soulless steed a kick. She raced through the air at me, and I stepped aside a moment too late, the hag's left shoulder catching mine and throwing me to the ground once more. With an unearthly cackle, she rocketed skywards.

I stood up slowly and was just tying a bow on my string of invectives when my speech was cut short by the sight of something even more horrid than the witch. A heap of—What were they? Human heads?—was racing up the path towards me. Even in the darkness of the night, I could see that not only was the mob moving quickly but also, as the heads tumbled over one another, they seemed to be transforming. At one moment they appeared to be the countenances of decrepit men, their howling mouths and dark eye-sockets as folded and hollow as the stumps of dead, storm-blasted trees. Then the old men's keening gave way to a celestial sort of song as the wrinkled tumult was replaced by a cascade of round, healthy faces of young women, each of them made up for a sumptuous night on the town and all of them singing as they came flying towards me.

I was beginning to think this monster might not be so terrible after all, if its faces were to keep looking like that. But just as the jumble reached me, they changed once more, this time into a pile of leathery, distinctly recognisable visages. Not that I needed to see them to make out who they were, for the coarse voices of the horrific heads matched precisely those of the workmen at the stone wall.

Then they were upon me, and I fell again to earth, my hands across my face. The barks of the ghastly workmen drowned out all thought, and their tumbling over my body, like so many cabbages rolling from an upturned cart, gave way to something different. Now among the heads were many strong arms, and I felt myself jostled, pawed at, and then gathered straight up into the stinking, barbarous multitude until I was completely engulfed.

My heart already in my shoes, I nonetheless surmised that the unholy mob, and I along with it, was ascending rapidly away from the surface of the earth. No head-scratching was required, as it were, to tell me then exactly what was going on, or into whose sweaty, grubby hands I'd fallen this evening. This was a fly-by from the most notorious members of the Unseelie Court, the wind-riding host of restless Faerie spirits known in the Highlands as the *Sluagh*. I was utterly theirs now, aloft and helpless in their clutches.

As we continued to rise, four particularly rough arms took hold of me. Two of them interlocked with my elbows, as if in some rude duplication of a country dance, and another two took hold of my legs. I ventured a glance down and realised that my suspicions were correct. The initial shock of the assault had left me shaken, but now, seeing the ground speed by beneath us some quarter of a mile distant, my senses were well and truly jangled.

One thing was clear enough, though—a terrible fate would be mine should I not break free from the icy grip of the Sluagh. What did they want with me? Would I be dropped to my death from this great height? Or if I wasn't, would I be carried to an accursed place for participation in unspeakable rites? It was with this train of thought hurtling through my mind that I began to push—with great difficulty, for the evil fairies' grip was firm—my right arm across the front of my body in the direction of the object which contained my only hope for salvation.

Through decades of careful scientific application, I have developed a technique which I believe to be unique among all Faerie investigators. Their esteemed number is rife with those claiming access to what we all know as the Second Sight. Of course, anyone who actually possesses such a talent makes no distinction between it and the everyday sight which assists one in tying one's own shoes. The Second Sight cannot be turned on and off like a light-switch. It simply *is*, meaning whatever hobs or gremlins creep into the possessor's line of sight are perceived, there, plain as day. Romantics may dream of discovering ways of grabbing hold of this ability, of claiming the Second Sight for themselves. They can have it, for all I care. If I could grasp the Second Sight and bottle it up, I'd toss it into the sea.

It's an apt metaphor because I *have* succeeded in bottling, in a way, the means of bringing on in myself a talent related and in many ways superior to the Second Sight, and one which could help me escape my windborne captors. When in the presence of the fey, and having consumed a sufficient quantity of alcohol, I am able to bring on a form of seeing distinct from both standard vision and the Second Sight. Whereas my fellow fairy seers are capable of witnessing the phantasmagorical in the everyday, my advanced brand of clairvoyance takes things full circle, bringing on a vision devoid of wonder, stripped of the fantastic, even under the most fairy-riddled of circumstances. I speak, dear friend, of the exceptionally practical talent known as *the Third Sight*.

Heaven knows I was nearly drunk enough. If only I could reach my flask.

The Sluagh's grip upon my limbs remained strong, and the flying host seemed to pick up speed.

Despite telling myself not to look, I found my gaze wandering earthwards. Not far ahead I could see the clusters of house lights lining the long edges of Loch Ness. Were the Sluagh planning to drown me, to offer me in sacrifice to the serpent coiled beneath the frigid waves? I drove these thoughts from my mind, focusing all attention on my effort to reach the flask in my jacket's inner pocket. With extraordinary effort, for the disembodied arms were stout, I reached it just as we crossed over the shoreline, untwisted the cap with my teeth, and drank down every last ounce of whisky within.

My shout of triumph must have unnerved my abductors, for we began quickly to descend. The black mirror of Loch Ness raced up to meet us, and my stomach felt a sick rush. The host shifted their grip on me until I was face down, my nose skimming the loch's dark, glassy surface.

My time had surely reached its end. The whisky I'd drunk had come too late to dispel these devils, and now I was moments from an inglorious death, about to be dropped like a stylishly appointed stone into the depths of the Ness. I was surprised at how lucid my thoughts were at that moment and how clearly, too, shone my own reflection in the lake's still waters. To look into the abyss is one thing, but to see in it not some grim harvester of souls but one's own face is, I will have to hope, more terrifying still. For it was not Death I saw looking back at me, but my own horrified visage. And then, blackness.

Reports from people who've returned from the verge of shuffling off their mortal coil regularly include mentions of a white light. I now know with certainty that this brilliant beam is no legend. Had I not thought that some hope for the survival of my soul lay beyond the searing brightness which cut, razor-like, into my field of vision, then I must say I would have preferred to keep on with the darkness which had enveloped me what seemed like a moment before.

The light pulsated with intensity, now growing, now fading, now growing again. It seemed to be keeping time with the heavy, burning sensation thrumming throughout the whole of my body, mainly in the head region. If I could join the light, my reasoning went, I might be able to cast aside this pain-wracked physical form, to step into the afterlife, to know bliss.

I heard a faraway door open, and panic seized my heart. My mind sensed the presence of a gatekeeper, a mystical toll collector who would demand proof of my worthiness. There wasn't a moment to lose. I quickly began preparing a rhetorical defence for any transgressions of morality I may have enacted in life. I was just formulating a good line of explanation regarding the unfortunate incident of the jar of Bovril and the family dog roundabout my sixth birthday, when the unseen angel of judgment spoke.

"Reginald." Its voice a bludgeon.

"But Horatio liked it at first!" I blurted, opening wide my eyes as I did. The white light punished my senses, and I could hear the terrible angel laugh a booming laugh. I writhed and, realising I was lying beneath a sort of soft, sweet-smelling coverlet, pulled it up round my blistering head.

"There you are, old bean." It was Marcus. "Stay where you are, and rest. I've brought you some toast and a little splash of something."

I peeked out feebly from beneath the blanket, shutting my eyes only after I'd noted the location of the silver tray and cup on the nightstand. The professor was a right alchemist when it came to brewing a morning-after remedy. I resolved to reach for this one as soon as I felt my faculty for extending my arms had returned to 50 percent. In my estimation, this occurrence would take place sometime around Wednesday of next week.

"You never fail to impress me with your lust for life, Mr. Bakeley," Marcus continued in a mercifully soft tone. "I knew you'd find a visit to Felstane diverting. It's a good thing I was returning home a bit late myself. I heard your shouts coming from the shore just south of the house. My dear boy, you looked as though you were about to crawl into the loch! Did you fancy going round to Nessie's for a nightcap?"

I groaned. The professor could do with speaking a touch softer still.

"No matter now," he went on. "I'm glad I found you, and I do believe you'll be all right, once you're out of the grip of last night's demons. Be glad you weren't at my meeting. After all the usual tedious discussions and a bit of new business regarding unexpectedly heavy fairy migrations this season, we all attempted our annual photograph. Took us ten minutes just to settle on who ought to stand where! Utter chaos. Mob rule, if you know what I mean."

I had a sense.

"And I found this on the shore as well." I ventured a glimpse in the direction of Marcus's voice and watched in surprise as he set the yellow cat's-eye marble next to the cup, the heavy glass thing touching down on the silver tray with a resounding clank. "It's yours now, and I'd hate for you to lose it."

The last thing I wanted to see was that baleful marble, but in my condition I was helpless to protest. I would have to find a way to slip it back into the vase in the front hall before my departure.

Marcus began to turn towards the door to the hallway, then stopped. "Ah! There was one more thing I knew I had to tell you. Nearly forgot. You received a telephone call about an hour ago. There was a gentleman on the line who asked for you, and I'll be damned if his voice wasn't *exactly* like yours. At first I thought it was you, playing some sort of

trick on me. He wouldn't leave a name or a number—said he'd try again some other time. It was the
oddest thing, Reginald. Isn't life strange?"

And with the thunder of the professor's footsteps ringing in my ears as he made his way down
the echoing hall, I had to agree that indeed it was.

RESOURCES

Stockists

Brownie Abatement (Fine Stationery)

Frank Smythson Ltd
40, New Bond Street
London W1Y 0DE

Brownie Abatement (Tailoring)

Gieves & Hawkes Ltd
1, Savile Row
London W1S 3JR

Flower-Fairy Collecting

Anglian Lepidopterist Supplies
Station Road
Hindolveston
Norfolk NR20 5DE

Flower-Fairy Management

National Vegetable Society
Bracklinn
14 Dronley Road
Birkhill
Dundee DD2 5QD

Gnoming Outfitters

Holland & Holland
33 Bruton Street
London W1J 6HH

J. Barbour & Sons Ltd
Simonside
South Shields
Tyne and Wear NE34 9PD

James Purdey & Sons Ltd
Audley House
57–58 South Audley Street
London W1K 2ED

The Sporting Lodge
Storth
Milnthorpe
Cumbria LA7 7JA

Pixie-Proof Rambling (Walking Sticks)

James Smith & Sons
53 New Oxford Street
London WC1A 1BL

Trolling Outfitters

Atkin Grant & Lang
Windmill Road
Markyate
St Albans
Hertfordshire AL3 8LP

Organisations

Druidry

The Order of Bards, Ovates and Druids
Post Office Box 1333
Lewes
East Sussex BN7 1DX

Elf-Shot Gathering

Council for British Archaeology
St Mary's House
66 Bootham
York YO30 7BZ

Freemasonry

United Grand Lodge of England
Freemason's Hall
60 Great Queen Street
London WC2B 5AZ

Rambling

Ordnance Survey
Adanac Drive
Southampton SO16 0AS

Ramblers
2nd Floor Camelford House
87–90 Albert Embankment
London SE1 7TW

FURTHER READING

Allen, Darina. *Forgotten Skills of Cooking.* Kyle Cathie, 2009.

Brickell, Christopher. *Royal Horticultural Society Encyclopedia of Plants and Flowers.* Dorling Kindersley, 2010.

Collins. *Letter Writing: How to Get Results.* Harper-Collins UK, 2004.

Fearnley-Whittingstall, Hugh. *The River Cottage Cookbook.* HarperCollins, 2001.

Hart-Davis, Duff. *Fauna Britannica.* Weidenfeld & Nicolson, 2002.

Hendry, George. *Midges in Scotland.* Aberdeen University Press, 1989.

Miller, Judith. *Miller's Antiques Handbook & Price Guide.* Miller's Publications, 2012.

Phillips, Roger. *Mushrooms and Other Fungi of Great Britain and Europe.* Pan Books, 1981.

Russ, Mel. *Sea Angling from Kent to Cornwall.* Hutchinson, 1990.

Swan, Mike. *Rough Shooting*. Swan Hill Press, 2007.

Thear, Katie. *Starting with Chickens*. Broad Leys Publishing Company, 1999.

Watkins, Alfred. *The Old Straight Track*. Abacus, 1988.

ABOUT REGINALD BAKELEY

REGINALD BAKELEY is best known for his long-standing editorship of *Phooka, The Journal of the Overland Mallet Club*. An avid sportsman and defender of rural life, Bakeley has devoted himself to public awareness and management of fairy populations throughout Britain. He maintains a website at *www.goblinproofing.com*.

ABOUT CLINT MARSH

CLINT MARSH is a writer and publisher of practical esoterica. He has served as Reginald Bakeley's American editor since 1998, distributing Bakeley's conservation-minded pamphlets about the Fairy Kingdom through Wonderella Printed. Learn more about Marsh and his practical esoterica at his website, *www.wonderella.org*.